BARRON'S BOOK NOTES

GEORGE ORWELL'S
1984

BY

Kit Reed
Visiting Professor of English
Wesleyan University

SERIES EDITOR

Michael Spring
Editor, *Literary Cavalcade*
Scholastic Inc.

BARRON'S EDUCATIONAL SERIES, INC.
Woodbury, New York / London / Toronto / Sydney

ACKNOWLEDGMENTS

We would like to acknowledge the many painstaking hours of work Holly Hughes and Thomas F. Hirsch have devoted to making the *Book Notes* series a success.

© Copyright 1984 by Barron's Educational Series, Inc.

All inquiries should be addressed to:
Barron's Educational Series, Inc.
113 Crossways Park Drive
Woodbury, New York 11797

Library of Congress Catalog Card No. 84-18432

International Standard Book No. 0-8120-3449-X

Library of Congress Cataloging in Publication Data
Reed, Kit.
  George Orwell's 1984.

  (Barron's book notes)
  Bibliography: p. 115
  Summary: A guide to reading "1984" with a critical and appreciative mind. Includes background on the author's life and times, sample tests, term paper suggestions, and a reading list.
    1. Orwell, George, 1903–1950. 1984. [1. Orwell, George, 1903–1950. 1984. 2. English literature—History and criticism] I. Title   II. Series.
PR6029.R8N66   1984   823'.912   84-18432
ISBN 0-8120-3449-X (pbk.)

PRINTED IN THE UNITED STATES OF AMERICA

456   550   987654321

CONTENTS

ADVISORY BOARD

HOW TO USE THIS BOOK

You have to know how to approach literature in order to get the most out of it. This *Barron's Book Notes* volume follows a plan based on methods used by some of the best students to read a work of literature.

Begin with the guide's section on the author's life and times. As you read, try to form a clear picture of the author's personality, circumstances, and motives for writing the work. This background usually will make it easier for you to hear the author's tone of voice, and follow where the author is heading.

Then go over the rest of the introductory material—such sections as those on the plot, characters, setting, themes, and style of the work. Underline, or write down in your notebook, particular things to watch for, such as contrasts between characters and repeated literary devices. At this point, you may want to develop a system of symbols to use in marking your text as you read. (Of course, you should only mark up a book you own, not one that belongs to another person or a school.) Perhaps you will want to use a different letter for each character's name, a different number for each major theme of the book, a different color for each important symbol or literary device. Be prepared to mark up the pages of your book as you read. Put your marks in the margins so you can find them again easily.

Now comes the moment you've been waiting for—the time to start reading the work of literature. You may want to put aside your *Barron's Book*

Notes volume until you've read the work all the way through. Or you may want to alternate, reading the *Book Notes* analysis of each section as soon as you have finished reading the corresponding part of the original. Before you move on, reread crucial passages you don't fully understand. (Don't take this guide's analysis for granted—make up your own mind as to what the work means.)

Once you've finished the whole work of literature, you may want to review it right away, so you can firm up your ideas about what it means. You may want to leaf through the book concentrating on passages you marked in reference to one character or one theme. This is also a good time to reread the *Book Notes* introductory material, which pulls together insights on specific topics.

When it comes time to prepare for a test or to write a paper, you'll already have formed ideas about the work. You'll be able to go back through it, refreshing your memory as to the author's exact words and perspective, so that you can support your opinions with evidence drawn straight from the work. Patterns will emerge, and ideas will fall into place; your essay question or term paper will almost write itself. Give yourself a dry run with one of the sample tests in the guide. These tests present both multiple-choice and essay questions. An accompanying section gives answers to the multiple-choice questions as well as suggestions for writing the essays. If you have to select a term paper topic, you may choose one from the list of suggestions in this book. This guide also provides you with a reading list, to help you when you start research for a term paper, and a selection of provocative comments by critics, to spark your thinking before you write.

THE AUTHOR AND HIS TIMES

Two days before he died, the author of *1984* left a will saying that he wanted no biography written. Like most novelists, he wanted his work judged for and by itself. This is ironic, since few novels reflect the author's progress through life—and the stormy political climate of his times—as clearly as George Orwell's *1984*. Most Orwell scholars see the life as a logical "road to *1984*." Knowing about Orwell's life, therefore, will help you know the novel.

Orwell began life with the name Eric Blair. He was born in India in 1903, the son of what he called a "lower-upper-middle class" family. For the author, this was an important distinction. The term meant that he came from the same social background as the landed gentry but was set apart by the fact that his family had very little money. His father worked for the British government in India, where he could live well on less money. Like most British officials, he sent the family back to England to spare them the hardships of the heat and of the monsoon season.

Growing up in Henley-on-Thames, west of London, Eric knew by the time he was four or five that he wanted to be a writer. Like his character Winston Smith in *1984*, he thought of himself as an outsider and a rebel. He told one childhood friend: "You are noticed more if you are standing on your head than if you are right side up."

At eight, he was packed off to boarding school at St. Cyprian's, where he was more of an outsider than ever, as a lone scholarship student among wealthy children. The schoolmaster and his wife used kicks and caresses to keep the boys in line. This was Eric's first taste of dictatorship, of being helpless under the rule of an absolute power. Orwell transfers these feelings to Winston, who in *1984* finds himself trapped in a harsh totalitarian system.

In an essay called "Such, Such were the Days," Orwell writes about being beaten for wetting his bed. The masters were quick to point out, whenever he got into trouble, that he was a "charity" student. They found him difficult and unresponsive. Like most lonely children, Eric consoled himself by making up stories in his head, and holding imaginary conversations with himself.

Later Orwell wrote that during his first twenty-five years he was writing, and living, a continuing story in his head. He began as a Robin Hood-like figure, starring in imaginary adventures. Later he became the careful observer, trying to describe what was going on around him as accurately as possible. This seems very like Winston in *1984*—a man who commits crimes in his head while outwardly obeying Party orders.

At Eton, a prestigious public school (equivalent to U.S. private or prep schools), Blair wrote some verse and worked on school magazines. Once again a scholarship student, he remained an outsider. In the years immediately following World War I, he was part of the antinomian movement at Eton, committed to overturning current standards and belief. Although he was against religion, Blair was confirmed in the Anglican Church, or Church of England, along with the rest of his classmates. Later he would be married and buried in Anglican ceremonies.

When his classmates went on to Oxford or Cambridge, Eric was faced with a decision. He could not afford to go to a university and his grades kept him from winning any more scholarships. He may have been sick of studying. And so he decided to join the Indian Imperial Police, a British force assigned to keep order in British dependencies. This pleased his father, who had rejoined the family in England. With the blessings of the family, Eric went out to Burma for a five-year hitch.

Later he wrote of this experience, "In Moulmein, in Lower Burma, I was hated by large numbers of people. . . ." Life must have been difficult for an aspiring writer, who was employed to keep order in a foreign country in the name of the British empire. Eric hated the police and everything they stood for; he often hated the people he was supposed to help, and he hated the things he was called upon to do in the name of his country. He felt isolated, lonely and deserted. You'll see how he uses this sense of guilt and isolation in portraying Winston Smith, who feels guilty about working for the ruling Party.

Orwell claimed later that his spell in Burma ruined his health. His lungs had always troubled him, and in 1927 he was sent back to England on a convalescent leave. That year he resigned from the police and dedicated himself to becoming a writer. His father never quite forgave him.

An avid reader whose favorite writers included futurist H.G. Wells (*War of the Worlds*) and satirist Jonathan Swift (*Gulliver's Travels*), Blair began reading and writing in earnest. He was excited by *The People of the Abyss*, by Jack London, who had gone "down and out," putting on rags and living among the destitute, the underclass, so he could write a book about them.

Blair decided to go "down and out" too—partly because he was trying to gather material, and partly because he wanted to erase the guilt and disgust he felt for serving in the Indian Imperial Police and for being a member of the privileged class. He bought tramps' clothes from a second-hand store and began a five-year period in which he lived, off and on, among tramps in flophouses. He took odd jobs and lived on pennies, first in London and then in Paris. Although he had begun to write for periodicals, he eventually ran out of money. Broke and desperate, he ended up with pneumonia in the paupers' ward in a French hospital.

During his "down and out" period, Blair learned what life was like for the underclass—desperate people with little hope for a decent future. Unlike them, however, he had a comfortable home to retreat to. You'll read in *1984* that Winston goes among the underclass, or *proles,* but can't or won't join them. Perhaps Orwell believed too strongly in class divisions to deny them completely.

Writing about his "down and out" experiences, Blair did what most good writers do: he transformed and fused what had happened to him to build a coherent story. The book went through several versions. He was about to give up on it when a friend took the manuscript to an agent who found him a publisher.

Down and Out in Paris and London was first published in 1933. Blair chose a pseudonym because, he said, "I am not proud of it." On paper, at least, he became George Orwell. Although friends and family continued to call him "Eric," he was George Orwell to everybody who read and wrote about him. In time he thought of having his name legally changed. If Eric Blair was the little boy who was lonely at school and who, in Burma, did things he was not proud of,

George Orwell was the writer with a cause. That cause defined itself in the 1930s.

By this time he was teaching school. Though he attracted several women, he was a late-bloomer socially and apparently he was never quite at ease with women. According to those who knew Orwell, he neither understood nor liked women very well, a fact that may have influenced his drawing of women characters—including Julia, Winston's lover in *1984*.

This did not prevent his falling in love with Eileen O'Shaughnessy in 1935. As soon as he met her at a party, he knew he wanted to marry her. Schoolteaching was not for him, though, and he had moved to London and worked in a bookstore. He had just published *Burmese Days*, his first novel, and was at work on *A Clergyman's Daughter*. (His novel about his bookstore days would be called *Keep the Aspidistra Flying*.)

The year 1936 was perhaps the most important in Orwell's life. In January, his publisher, a founder of the Left Wing Book Club, commissioned him to live among the unemployed coal miners in the north of England and write a book about their lives. The publisher hoped to awaken the English to their poverty and suffering so that people would act to change conditions.

According to friends, Orwell went north without preconceptions. In Burma he had learned what evils an absolute government can do even when it's trying to help people. His "down and out" days had taught him about class divisions and the horrors of poverty. Living among the poor in Northern England, he underwent a socialist conversion. Recognizing the plight of the poor was not enough, though; he had to urge the public to do something about it. And so he wrote *The Road To Wigan Pier*, alerting the public to the harsh lives of these people.

That summer George and Eileen married and went to live above a country store in an English village. While Eileen, a trained psychologist, got stuck tending the store, Orwell wrote. Their honeymoon ended dramatically with the outbreak of civil war in Spain, where Francisco Franco and his Spanish generals were trying to overthrow the brand-new people's government.

Idealists from all over the world were going to Spain to help the new government, which had only recently taken the place of a monarchy. They saw Franco's fascists as threatening the cause of freedom and democracy everywhere. Meanwhile, in Germany, the Nazi party under Adolph Hitler was in complete power. Hitler was rattling his weapons, preparing a bid to take over Europe. In Russia, the people's revolution had done away with the czarist ruling class, but under Stalin, the Communist government threatened the freedom of the people. Stalin was engaged in purging his enemies from the party. Both these totalitarian powers were now aiding Franco. Orwell saw this as an opportunity to live out his ideals and went to Spain to fight for the "Popular Front" government.

The political thicket Orwell waded into was so complex that historians are still trying to untangle it. There were several parties fighting Franco; alliances kept changing. Orwell was excited by what appeared to be a classless society in Barcelona. To help preserve it, he joined one of the splinter parties fighting Franco and went to the front to fight.

By the time he returned to Barcelona six months later, everything had changed. The classless society had vanished; the rich were back in power. The party he had joined was out of favor and he was in danger of being purged. Riots and street fighting raged. History rewrote itself as he watched. Although it would be eight years before Orwell found the vocabulary to transform the nightmare into a novel, these experiences paved the way to *1984*. Injured by a sniper's bullet, Orwell left Spain disillusioned by the sad end of the Popular Front's efforts: Franco would take over the country. Orwell was convinced that Stalinism, which purged political enemies for the "good" of the state, was as dangerous as Nazism. He was also certain that he must fuse his politics and his art.

He would become a political reformer, trying to change the world through his writing. In "Why I Write," he says, "Every line of serious work that I have written since 1936 has been written, directly or indirectly, *against* totalitarianism and *for* democratic socialism, as I understand it."

Orwell was a democratic Socialist who believed in a centralized government that would take over such things as medical care and running the railroads for the good of the people, bringing benefits to all. At the same time, he believed this government should be run by the people. This was, he believed, the fine line Great Britain must tread—doing what was best for the people without hampering their freedom.

At the time, he believed Britain could do this while staying out of the impending clash with Hitler. During this period in the late 1930s, Hitler prepared to make war, while in Russia, Stalin got rid of his enemies through a series of political purges. Hitler and Stalin were allied. Orwell finished his book about the Spanish experience, and called it *Homage to Catalonia*. Ill again, he went with Eileen to Morocco to recuperate.

Meanwhile, Hitler marched on Poland, on Holland, on Belgium, on France. Britain's entry into World War II in 1940 was inevitable and marked the end of Orwell's brief period as a pacifist. He enlisted in the Home Guard because his health prevented his joining the armed forces.

Later Orwell wrote propaganda for the BBC, an education in how to know one thing yet say another for the good of the people. As you'll see, this training foreshadowed Winston's job in the Ministry of Truth. England was under attack by air, and buzz bombs, Nazi V-2 rockets, exploded on London almost daily until the war ended. Every day people lived with death and danger and shortages of food and clothing. Russia, which had begun the war as Germany's ally, took up arms against Hitler, grappling with the Nazis at Stalingrad. History, then, laid the groundwork for *1984*, in which major powers are always at war but the enemy keeps changing.

By 1944 Orwell was finishing *Animal Farm*, a parable about Stalinism. Because the Soviet Union was now a British ally, he had a hard time getting it published. Besides that, he was ill again. Eileen needed surgery but they put it off because of expense. In the final days of the war he went to Paris and Germany as a war correspondent. He was hospitalized again. While he was in Germany Eileen died in surgery, leaving him with an infant son they had adopted. Grieving and ill, he came home to begin another novel. This would be his last.

Publication of *Animal Farm* brought Orwell recognition and freedom from financial pressure. An enemy of totalitarianism, he saw what he thought were totalitarian tendencies in the British government. He took a country house on a remote island where he lived off and on while writing this final work, originally titled

"The Last Man in Europe." Sick as he was, he put off going to the hospital until he had a first draft finished. His doctor said, "If he ceases to try to get well and settles down to write another book he is almost certain to relapse quickly."

But Orwell had a mission. He wanted 1984 to be "a showup of the perversions to which a centralized society is liable, and which have already been realized in Communism and Fascism." He feared for Britain. Struggling against enormous physical odds (as Winston struggles under torture), he went home to finish a second draft. "The striking thing," he said of his increasing weakness, "is the contrast between the apparent normality of the mind and its helplessness when you attempt to get anything on paper."

Once more he put off treatment in order to make a final typescript. He had broken his health but he had finished the novel that would outlive him by generations. Hospitalized, Orwell saw the novel published in 1949. It was widely praised in a postwar world that had awakened to the realities of the Cold War in which there are no friends, only friendly enemies. It was taken as a chilling warning by readers who lived with the daily possibility of absolute nuclear destruction, a possibility which had been raised by the explosion of atomic bombs over Hiroshima and Nagasaki, Japan, in the last days of World War II.

Unlike his hero, Winston Smith, who was defeated by the society and by his own weakness, George Orwell ended his life with a triumph.

It is useful to remember that every writer uses real life for material, but only the best writers learn how to *transform* it into living fiction. With intelligence and skill, they take what they know to create what they don't know, making something so real that it is truer than real life. In *1984*, George Orwell has done this brilliantly. Because he was a wonderful novelist before he became a political reformer, he had the skill to make his message known all over the world.

BIG BROTHER IS WATCHING YOU, say the posters in Orwell's novel. His warning has passed into the language.

THE NOVEL

The Plot

In the near future of 1984, the world is divided into three superpowers, which are always at war. In battered London—a part of Oceania—middle-aged Winston Smith works as a minor member of the ruling Party, under the leadership of all-seeing, all-powerful Big Brother. He lives under the eye of a TV monitor. If he does anything out of order, a voice barks out instructions. The trouble is that the Party frowns on art, on sex, on the life of the mind—in fact, on everything except Party business, hatred of the Party's enemies, and love of Big Brother.

Every Party member knows the worst crime of all is *Thoughtcrime:* having evil thoughts against the Party or Big Brother. BIG BROTHER IS WATCHING YOU, warn the posters.

As Winston's story opens he's committing a crime in spite of Big Brother. Troubled by dreams and memories of better times, inspired by secret glances from O'Brien, a member of the powerful Inner Party, Winston is starting a diary. Practically the first thing he writes is a major offense: DOWN WITH BIG BROTHER.

At work in the Ministry of Truth, Winston alters books and periodicals to keep up with the changing Party history. Oceania is allied with Eastasia in war against Eurasia—but were they always? Rebel leader Emmanuel Goldstein is the public enemy in the daily Two Minutes of Hate—but was he always? Three enemies of the Party confessed and repented their

Thoughtcrimes—did they really? Troubled by questions and memory flashes, Winston retreats to the "down and out" or *prole* (short for proletarian) neighborhoods, where the lower classes breed and squabble without Party interference. He spends happy hours in the second-hand store where he bought the diary.

Meanwhile Winston is afraid the dark-haired girl from the Fiction Department where he works is going to turn him in for *Thoughtcrime*. He's certain O'Brien is a secret enemy of the Party. To his astonishment, the dark-haired girl slips him a note: I LOVE YOU. Julia wants to meet. They go to the *prole* sector to begin an affair, another crime against the state. Winston is seduced not only by Julia but by the idea of rebellion. He and Julia continue their affair in a private room above the second-hand store. He thinks it's love like theirs that will eventually destroy the Party.

What Winston most hopes for happens. He gets a message from O'Brien. At night he and Julia go to O'Brien's lavish home and swear they'll do anything they can to help O'Brien's secret group, The Brotherhood, to overthrow the Party.

Winston's determination is strengthened by a sudden political change: Oceania is no longer at war with Eurasia, now Eurasia is at war with Eastasia. Eurasia is the ally. According to Big Brother it has always been this way, so Winston has to change all the records to make this true.

In the midst of his despair and confusion, he has one thing to cling to. O'Brien has given him a forbidden book by Goldstein, the enemy of the Party. Winston takes the book to his secret room and begins to read the extensive writing on Party philosophy. When Julia comes, he reads it aloud to her. By the time he's finished, she's asleep. After dozing, Winston goes to the window to watch a huge *prole* mother singing as she hangs out the wash for her enormous family. He is thinking that the *proles* are the hope of the future when suddenly his world collapses.

Within seconds the Thought Police crash in. Winston's nice landlord is not what he seems. Neither is O'Brien. Winston is held prisoner and tortured in the Ministry of Love, where O'Brien spends months trying to brainwash him. The final step comes when O'Brien takes Winston to Room 101, where that which he most fears is waiting. As a cage of rats closes over his face, he forgets everything, even his love for Julia. His spirit is broken. As the novel ends, Winston is back at work, his affair ended and his diary destroyed, along with his memories and the last fragments of his personality.

The State has triumphed. Winston has learned to love Big Brother.

The Characters

Not all the characters in *1984* are rounded individuals like Winston, Julia, and O'Brien. Many have parts like bit players in a stage play, carrying signboards that signal the author's intentions. If you look at them one by one, you'll be able to write about the difference between characters as people and characters as symbols, or emblems.

MAJOR CHARACTERS

Big Brother

To begin with, Big Brother is not a real person. All-present as he is, all-powerful and forever watching, he is seen only on TV. Although his picture glares out from huge posters that shout, BIG BROTHER IS WATCHING YOU, nobody sees Big Brother in person.

Orwell had several things in mind when he created Big Brother. He was certainly thinking of Russian leader Joseph Stalin; the pictures of Big Brother even look like him. He was also thinking of Nazi leader Adolph Hitler and Spanish dictator Francisco Franco. Big Brother stands for all dictators everywhere. Orwell may have been thinking about figures in certain religious faiths when he drew Big Brother: the mysterious, powerful, God-like figure who sees and knows everything—but never appears in person.

For Inner Party members, Big Brother is a leader, a bogeyman they can use to scare the people, and their authorization for doing whatever they want. If anybody asks, they can say they are under orders from Big Brother.

For the unthinking proles, Big Brother is a distant authority figure.

For Winston, Big Brother is an inspiration. Big Brother excites and energizes Winston, who hates him. He is also fascinated by Big Brother and drawn to him in some of the same ways that he is drawn to O'Brien, developing a love-hate response to both of them that leads to his downfall.

Winston Smith

Orwell named his hero after Winston Churchill, England's great leader during World War II. He added the world's commonest last name: Smith. The ailing, middle-aged rebel can be considered in many different lights.

1. You'll have to decide for yourself whether Winston is a hero in his secret battle with Big Brother, or

whether he's only a sentimental man with a death wish, who courts his death openly through an illegal love affair and through his alliance with the enemies of Big Brother.

    a. If Winston is a 20th-century hero, it seems logical for him to keep a diary even though he knows it will hang him. It is right for him to follow his heart and have an affair with Julia. He is doing the only possible thing by seeking out O'Brien and joining the Brotherhood, which is committed to overthrowing Big Brother. Naturally he will defy authorities even after he is captured and tortured, trying to keep one last shred of personality intact.

    b. If he's so heroic, why is he so foolhardy? It makes no sense for him to create a permanent love-nest when he knows it will speed his capture. "It was as though they were intentionally stepping nearer to their graves," he thinks. A careful man would never open up to O'Brien without knowing whether he is to be trusted. You can argue that Winston's continuing defiance of the Party after his capture is one more way of courting disaster. Do you think Winston secretly enjoys torture? Although he confesses to everything they want him to, he extends the torture by continuing his inner defiance—something the Party seems to know. Winston's thoughts in *Part Two, Section IV*, point to this interpretation.

  2. You can learn more about Winston by considering his view of sex as a means of rebellion. He's divorced because his wife couldn't produce the baby the Party expects, and wouldn't consider sex for any other purpose because desire is *Thoughtcrime*. He is drawn to Julia because she is "corrupt," which means she enjoys sex and has previously taken several lovers. Knowing he will be punished, he falls in love with her. Winston's ideal partner for the future is not Julia, but the mountainous *prole* woman who hangs out the laundry for her many children. Another of Winston's ideal women, whom Winston writes about in his diary, is the refugee mother protecting her child with her own body. Orwell may be arguing that woman-as-mother is to be honored, but any other kind of love is to be punished.

3. Is the real love affair in Winston's mind, and is it with O'Brien? O'Brien is on Winston's mind in *Part One, Section I*. Winston dreams about him in *One, Section II*, when O'Brien says, "We shall meet in the place where there is no darkness." In *Three, I*, this dream is fulfilled in an astonishing way. Does O'Brien stand for hope or for the fulfillment of Winston's death wish? Does he seek him out precisely to bring about his capture? Look at *Part Three, Sections I, II, III and IV*, where Winston is captured and brainwashed. He doesn't hate or resist O'Brien. Instead the two minds are locked in a bizarre courtship. Winston respects his destroyer as he never respects Julia.

4. Winston's ideas about class lines tell us something about his values, and Orwell's.

> **a.** Winston despises his middle-class neighbors, the Parsons. He bitterly resents and envies the lower classes because they are vital, physical and mindlessly happy. They are also slightly gross to him—particularly

the huge woman with the laundry. He sees the underclass as the hope for the future, yet recognizes that they have neither the brains nor the means to start a revolution. What's more, he doesn't like them well enough to join them, or even enough to disappear among them. Why doesn't he run away to the ghetto? BECAUSE HE IS NOT LIKE THEM.

b. O'Brien is his ideal, even after O'Brien starts brainwashing Winston. O'Brien is a member of the Inner Party, polished and sophisticated, and so high up in the organization that he enjoys a handsome, comfortable apartment and a servant. Does this reflect some hidden attitude of Orwell's that conflicts with his role as defender of the masses?

5. Nostalgia for the past is central to Winston's rebellion. He alone seems to remember that there was life before the Party; to remember the now vanished rural landscape, to pine for the mother he betrayed. The antique diary he buys; the old-fashioned paperweight that is central to the story; his recurring dreams and memories—all make him different. Is Winston really trying to design a new future, or does he want to get back into the past, where it's safe?

6. Some people think Winston is really George Orwell dressed up in a blue Party uniform. He seems to have some of Orwell's ailments, and many of the same worries, and he lives an active inner life as Orwell did at St. Cyprian's. On the other hand, Winston finally crumples under pressure from the Party, whereas Orwell fought illness to finish his stunning

novel. Do you think Winston is really only an extension of Orwell, or is he a full-blown character living a life of his own, in order that he can carry Orwell's warning about the dangers of totalitarianism to the public? You can argue either way.

Winston, as a character, is complex and troublesome because the author has used words to create a living, breathing person. Perhaps the most important question you'll decide for yourself is: Does this man deserve what happens to him? Could he have escaped if he had tried hard enough? Did he or did he not get what he wanted? Again, it's your decision.

Julia

Unlike Winston, Julia is basically a simple woman, something of a lightweight who loves her man and uses sex for fun as well as for rebellion. She is perfectly willing to accept the overnight changes in Oceania's history and doesn't trouble her pretty head about it. If Big Brother says black is white, fine. If he says two and two make five, no problem. She may not buy the Party line, but it doesn't trouble her. She falls asleep over Winston's reading of the treasured book by Goldstein. Revolutionary doctrine? Zzzzz. The act is enough for her; she doesn't need a rationale.

Orwell draws Winston's love object lovingly. Julia is all woman, sharp and funny as she is attractive, but she may also be a reflection of the author's somewhat limited view of the opposite sex. It might be useful to look at her more carefully. Is she the one-sided creation of a male author?

1. Julia may be lovable precisely because she stands for something forbidden. Perhaps the author thinks sexually active women are for fun, and only mothers are to be looked up to! Do the lovers Winston and Julia have much to talk about? (Read *Part Two, I, IV* and *V* before making up your mind.)

2.   Perhaps Julia is the practical realist, who knows that doctrine is bunk and that Winston is begging for trouble when he starts asking questions. She is the organizer, who approaches him and sets up a time and place for their meetings. She's the one who points out that they're going to be caught, and that when they are, they will confess and betray everything they care about—except each other. (Look at *Part Two, I, III, IV* for evidence to support this opinion.)

3.   Julia, not Winston, may be the true rebel. When O'Brien asks the couple whether they would betray all their principles to overthrow Big Brother, it's Julia who says she will never, ever give up Winston. (See *Part Two, VIII.*)

4.   Julia may be a weakling, the cause of Winston's downfall. Without the affair, he may have been able to keep his rebellion a secret. What would have happened if she hadn't tagged along to meet O'Brien? Julia does not lead the Thought Police to Winston, but without her, he would have been harder to catch. When the lovers are captured, it is Julia who betrays Winston right away. When they meet one last time at the end, it is Julia who is thick in the waist and dead in the heart and completely indifferent to him. (Read *Part Three, V.*)

Julia has many sides. Do they add up to a whole person? You'll have fun deciding.

O'Brien

Probably the most interesting thing about O'Brien is that we have only Winston's opinion of him. This burly but sophisticated leader of the Inner Party is supposed to be head of the secret Brotherhood dedicated to the overthrow of Big Brother. In his black coverall, he haunts both Winston's dreams and his waking moments to the very end of the novel.

1.   O'Brien may be a kind of super-being. He is certainly Winston's hope for the future as the novel opens. Winston's early reveries and his doglike devotion in *Part Two, VIII*, support this view. He seems to represent freedom and privilege to the downtrodden Winston. Even when Winston is in prison in Part Three, he is glad to see O'Brien. If the Thought Police are the "bad cops" after Winston's capture, O'Brien is the "good cop" who keeps Winston's confidence even as he destroys him. He's certainly Big Brother's mouthpiece, or preacher, as he explains Party doctrine to Winston in *Part Three, II–IV*.

2.   O'Brien may be rather a super-villain, who maliciously engineers Winston's downfall. After all, he seeks Winston out. He gives him the illegal Goldstein book, and it may be O'Brien's voice Winston hears from the TV set as he is captured at the end of Part Two. It is certainly O'Brien who brainwashes him, and O'Brien who takes Winston to the dreaded Room 101 to complete his "rehabilitation."

3.   Maybe O'Brien is a love object. Look again at Winston's doglike devotion at the end of Part Two, when he is caught. "It was starting," he thinks almost joyfully. "It was starting at last!" Look at the way O'Brien brainwashes Winston, from Section II in Part Three to the end. When he enters, Winston is almost

reassured. "Don't worry, Winston; you are in my keeping. . . . I shall save you. I shall make you perfect." Terrified as he is, Winston seems glad. From here to the finish, Winston and O'Brien are engaged in a delicate dance of life and death and, perhaps, love, that ends in Room 101, where Winston is confronted by that which he most fears. The experience changes him completely, and forever.

MINOR CHARACTERS

The minor characters in *1984* are not so much people as sign-carriers bearing Orwell's message. Everybody stands for something.

The Parsons Family
Winston's neighbors are drawn from the World War II days of the Hitler Youth when children were junior party members and so fired up by Nazism that they would even turn in their parents for speaking against the party. The Parsons children are on the lookout for Thoughtcrime. Their mother is scared to death of them. The father is the stereotypical dumb, zealous Party member who loves decorating the neighborhood for Hate Week and adores Big Brother. Watch what happens to him in Part Three, when the kids finally turn him in.

Mr. Charrington
The sweet old proprietor of the second-hand shop where Winston hides out loves antiques and talks about the old days in heartwarming tones. His antiques are not what they seem to be, and neither is Mr. Charrington. He is in fact a powerful member of the Thought Police and part of O'Brien's elaborate plot to snare Winston.

The Prole Woman

This great big lady has SYMBOL written all over her. Winston sees her as emblem of the hope for the future. She is like a brood mare standing out there doing her laundry, with her heavy, veined legs and her overblown female apparatus ready to drop babies to populate the future. The problem is that Orwell never explains how his uneducated and mindless *proles* can ever get their act together to make a revolution. Is this problem accidental, or is it one of the author's ironies, designed to sharpen his warning?

Winston's mother

This shadow figure appears only in Winston's dreams and memories. She stands for better days, for the past, and in a funny way for Winston's guilt. He survived; she didn't.

Syme

This Party member is too intelligent for his own good—another type. He is preparing a "Newspeak" dictionary, and he tells Winston—and us—that once the national vocabulary has been narrowed to a few hundred words, people won't be able to do or think bad things because they won't have words for them. Naturally he is purged.

Goldstein

Here's another type—the Trotsky of Oceania. Like the Russian revolutionary leader, he has been purged and has become a Party enemy. Some writers say Goldstein's book, which is quoted at length in Part Two, is a parody of political writings of the time, including a book by Leon Trotsky, a Russian revolutionary leader who had been purged. For Winston, Goldstein is the symbol of opposition to the Party— until he discovers who really wrote the book.

Old Man
Only the *proles* remember the past because nobody bothered to rewrite their history. This old drunk remembers, all right, but the bits are useless to Winston because all the old man can think about is his twitchy bladder and various shortages because he is "like the ant, which can see small objects and not large ones."

Jones, Aaronson, Rutherford
Three revolutionary leaders purged from the new Party. Only Winston remembers them.

Other Elements

SETTING

George Orwell's 1984 is set in Oceania in a city that's still named London, in a country called Airstrip One. The most important thing about the setting is that this is London in the *near future*. This remains true no matter what year you read the book.

In this near future, which is drawn from Orwell's imagination *and from conditions in London around World War II*, rocket bombs launched by some remote and unseen enemy (either Eurasia or Eastasia, according to Big Brother) explode here and there. All the buildings are delapidated. Victory Mansions, where Winston lives, is shabby and rundown. Even in the Ministry of Truth, where Winston works, everything is drab.

The most important physical element in almost every scene is the telescreen, which both watches citizens and gives war news, music, political speeches and messages from Big Brother. Everywhere are posters with Big Brother's picture, bearing the slogan:

BIG BROTHER IS WATCHING YOU.

THEME

Orwell's stated purpose dictates the major theme. He wants to warn people what can happen when governments are given too much power. He wants to show us how such governments can develop, and what methods they use to keep the people they are governing in their power. As you read THE CHARACTERS and THE STORY, a section-by-section discussion of *1984*, you'll find this major theme discussed at length, along with several other themes the author has developed.

1. AS WARNING AGAINST TOTALITARIAN GOVERNMENTS

You'll find the Party in Orwell's novel is all-powerful because it's run by a group whose major purpose is to gain and keep power. Their methods are harsh and efficient. They crush anybody who tries to commit an independent act (this includes keeping a diary or having an affair). Orwell describes the political history and psychological underpinnings in Goldstein's book, extracted at length in *Part Two, IX*.

2. AS DESCRIPTION OF TOTALITARIAN METHODS

We see how this works as we follow the story of Winston Smith—how the Party keeps watch over everybody and what methods it uses to keep individuals in line.

3. AS DESCRIPTION OF ONE MAN'S LONELINESS

Winston's memories of a happier past, his dreams and his hopes, lead him to fight the system. He seeks out O'Brien because he is lonely for somebody to talk to; this is spelled out in Part Three. In Part Two he has an affair with Julia, because he:

a. Is lonely and wants somebody to love.

b. Wants to fight the system through an illegal affair.

c. Is both lonely and wants to fight the system. (As you read Part Two, you can form arguments to support all these themes.)

4. AS DESCRIPTION OF WHAT HAPPENS TO ANYBODY WHO FAILS TO OBEY A TOTALITARIAN GOVERNMENT

In Part Three especially, this is spelled out as Winston is tortured and brainwashed. He is being punished for asking questions and for daring to have independent thoughts.

5. AS THE STORY OF ONE MAN BRINGING ON HIS OWN DOOM

Starting in Part One, when Winston begins the diary, reading through Part Two, in which he begins his affair and tries to contact the secret Brotherhood that opposes the Party, you'll find strong indications that Winston brings his capture and brainwashing on himself through defiant acts. Given the fact that his story has to end badly to emphasize Orwell's message of warning, you may believe Winston is being a brave rebel who would rather die than live under Party rule. It's also perfectly respectable to believe that Winston, in his loneliness, may be committing a form of suicide. A third way of looking at this is that Winston brings on his own capture, brainwashing, and conversion because in his heart he wants to be just like everybody else.

Remember that very few novels can be reduced to answers by-the-numbers. Good fictional characters, like Winston, are as well-rounded as real human beings, which means their moods and their motives are complicated and changeable. Your own personal responses and opinions are going to be important as you respond to George Orwell's novel.

STYLE

Orwell writes like many English novelists, with an eye for detail and the occasional comic touch. His style is basically clean and sharp and unornamented. He doesn't rely on numerous colorful adjectives and he doesn't overwrite. What he does do is choose the exact word to convey what he means at every step.

The long political excerpt from Goldstein's book, which occupies the second half of Part Two, is in a slightly different style. Orwell was using as his model political writings of his time, named in the discussion of Section IX in Part Two.

POINT OF VIEW

The novel *1984* is narrated in the third person, through a point-of-view character, Winston Smith. This means that Winston functions as the camera recording all the events. We see, hear and learn only what Winston can see, hear and learn, as it happens. We can see into Winston's thoughts and share his dreams and memories, but we see the other characters only as Winston sees them. We can't know anything Winston doesn't know, but since we are outside Winston's story, we can look at it and see danger when he doesn't—as when he goes openly to O'Brien's place in Part Two. We see what Winston sees but we also see Winston as he looks to others— something the character himself can't do.

At no point does the narrative point of view shift to any other character's mind. This is Winston's story from beginning to end.

FORM AND STRUCTURE

Although written as a novel of the near future, *1984* is not science fiction. It is a political parable, whose effectiveness comes: 1. from the author's ability to involve us so deeply in Winston's story that we care about him; 2. from the author's political convictions, his knowledge of political conditions, and his ability to project what might happen from what he already knows.

The novel *1984* is divided into three parts and an appendix.

Part One introduces Winston and his life in the near future, under the thumb of the ruling Party. It traces his first act of rebellion, and establishes his loneliness.

Part Two shows Winston trying to change his life by having a love affair with Julia, and meeting O'Brien, who he thinks is in a secret Brotherhood dedicated to overthrowing the Party. It shows his rising hopes for a better future being dashed by his capture. Part Two bulges because it contains a lengthy piece of political writing that may wreck the novel's structure, by bringing dramatic action to a complete halt.

Part Three details Winston's brainwashing by O'Brien, his resistance and eventual collapse, and his conversion to Party beliefs.

The Appendix contains a description of Newspeak. It is a kind of narrative leftover that didn't fit into the novel.

Notice that *1984* is one of the few novels with an appendix, the kind of thing you usually find in texts. Along with the political excerpt in Part Two, the Appendix advances the author's political message but may not help the book as novel. You may want to write about your approval of, or objection to, these extra sections.

The Story

What won't come across in any plot summary is the fact that, in addition to being both scary and prophetic, George Orwell's *1984* is a satiric novel, which means it's humorous, too. A look at any ten pages shows the wry and satiric way Orwell looks at things. Winston is a typical Englishman with a stiff upper lip and an eye for the grotesque. His story is more frightening than any melodrama precisely because it is funny. The novel falls in three parts.

PART ONE

SECTION I

Winston Smith, Party member and civil servant, comes home to the ramshackle Victory Mansions in the capital of Airstrip One, which used to be called England. The London of Orwell's near future is very like London after World War II, with its bombed-out buildings and its shortages and power failures. What's different are the posters of a huge face with eyes that seem to follow you everywhere, and bearing the legend:

BIG BROTHER IS WATCHING YOU.

He is. Winston knows it. A TV screen dominates his room, and in addition to bringing war news and exercise classes, the thing sees everything within range. It watches Winston. With today's TV monitoring systems and tactics learned from spy movies, we'd probably yawn and throw a blanket over it, but in Orwell's day this was big stuff. TV existed only in laboratory situations, and nobody had thought much about using it to *look at* things as well as to *show* them.

Winston is a small, skinny, middle-aged man wearing the blue Party coverall. He has fair hair and ruddy, chapped skin. He keeps his back to the screen in case the Thought Police tune in. From his window he can see the Ministry of Truth, where he works. On the building's face are lettered the Party slogans:

WAR IS PEACE
FREEDOM IS SLAVERY
IGNORANCE IS STRENGTH.

Was London always like this? Winston can't quite remember. What he knows is that the government is everywhere.

NOTE: For Orwell, an absolute government is something to hate and fear. He's trying to warn us against letting any government get this powerful. He communicates this warning through Winston, "the last (thinking) man in Europe."

Lighting a Victory cigarette and taking a slug of watery Victory gin, Winston unveils an antique book he bought illegally in a "free" store (one the Party does not run). Risking capture and death for committing a private act, he is about to begin a diary. His first entry is about a newsreel he has seen in which a gallant refugee mother protects her child from a helicopter attack on the boat they're in. This was a story written years before we saw film of the boat-people fleeing Viet Nam and Cambodia under fire.

NOTE: Winston's World and Ours

As you follow Winston, notice:

Which things are like conditions in our world today—wars at the fringes of the territory, for instance; totalitarian governments in Eastern Europe and Latin America; the presence of TV in every home to indoctrinate, if not to spy. Was Orwell a prophet or was he pushing events in his world of 1948 to their logical conclusion? Look for critical opinions at the end of this guide, and then decide for yourself.

Which things are different? Remember, Winston's future is our present. How powerful is our government, compared to the government of Oceania as portrayed in the pages to come? How are they alike? How different? On the basis of the first three sections, you'll be able to write about how Winston's life is different from ours, from his private life to his place in society and the role technology plays for him.

As he writes, Winston broods on his day at work. Who is the dark-haired girl, and why is she following him? What was O'Brien, the burly, urbane and powerful Inner Party member, doing in their sector during the Two Minutes' Hate today? Everybody in the section was taking out pent-up emotions on Emmanuel Goldstein, the rebel leader on the telescreen when Winston found himself distracted. (The Party uses Goldstein to focus members' hatred. Like the Nazis, the Party whips up anti-Jewish sentiment—Goldstein is a Jewish name—along with hatred for the superpower they're currently at war with. When everybody's hatred is at a high pitch, the Party channels this hatred into love for Big Brother.)

NOTE: The parts of the government of Oceania are:

Minitrue, the Ministry of Truth, or propaganda arm. This is where Winston works.

Minipax, the Ministry of Peace, which makes war.

Miniplenty, the Ministry of Plenty, which arranges shortages.

Miniluv, the hated and feared Ministry of Love, the center of secret Party activities. When he is captured, Winston will find out what happens here.

Today Winston was distracted by the nearness of the dark-haired girl, whom he hates because he wants her but knows he can't have her. Worse yet, in the few seconds before the Two Minutes' Hate wrought its inevitable magic and everybody present loved Big Brother, Winston hated Big Brother. He was even more excited because he caught O'Brien looking at him. "It was as though their two minds had opened and the thoughts were flowing one into the other through their eyes." He thinks O'Brien may be part of the Brotherhood pledged to overthrow Big Brother. Some readers believe Winston's real love affair in *1984* is with O'Brien. Watch them together in scenes to come and see what you think.

In a unique mixture of sex and politics, the Party channels sexual frustration to its own purposes. In Winston this channeling misfires. Lust and politics get all mixed up with the dark-haired girl, because, he now realizes, it's the Party's fault that he can't have her. He looks down and finds to his horror that he has been writing, over and over: DOWN WITH BIG BROTHER. He has committed the unforgivable— Thoughtcrime, as it's called in Newspeak. He knows his action will lead to capture and punishment. Thought Police will drag him away in the middle of the night (just the way Nazis in World War II took people to concentration camps). He will end up in the mysterious Ministry of Love, where terrible things happen to people who oppose Big Brother. He will be *vaporized*.

There is a knock at the door. Winston fears the worst.

NOTE: On Newspeak

In an Appendix at the end of the novel, Orwell describes Newspeak. It's the official language of Oceania, made to meet the needs of INGSOC, or English Socialism. When it becomes universal, Orwell tells us, nobody will be able to commit unwanted acts or think bad thoughts because actions and thoughts cannot exist without language to describe or define them. Example: "Free" will mean "without." A cat will be "free" of ticks, but people will no longer hanker for "freedom." Things will be "ungood" or "double plus ungood," but never bad. Orwell is playing with both words and politics. He asks us to believe that language affects life. You may disagree, but for the purposes of his story, Orwell asks us to believe that limiting vocabulary limits thought and action.

SECTION II

Instead of Thought Police, the person at Winston's door is his neighbor, Mrs. Parsons. Although Party members call one another *comrade*, this timid lady is very much a *Mrs*. Will Winston help her fix the plumbing? Her plump, patriotic husband is out on Party business. Winston is harassed by her monstrous children, who, in a patriotic fervor, accuse him of Thoughtcrime. They are Junior Spies.

NOTE: In World War II, Hitler Youth, indoctrinated from childhood, grew up to turn in their parents. Orwell uses the Parsons children as strong indicators of the dangerous political climate.

Depressed and anxious, Winston retreats to memories of a dream in which someone said, quietly, "We shall meet in the place where there is no darkness." He is sure it was the voice of O'Brien. And this is important: "Winston had never been able to feel sure . . . whether O'Brien was a friend or an enemy. Nor did it seem to matter greatly. There was a link of understanding between them. . . ." Yes, they will meet in the place where there is no darkness. In his loneliness and isolation, emotions which may mirror Eric Blair's loneliness in Burma, this hope is enough for Winston.

Writing in his diary, Winston reflects that this criminal act makes him a dead man. Look for echoes of this thought, especially as Part Two ends. His fatalism is interesting. Does this defiant act reflect high heroism or is it the result of a death wish? You can argue this either way, on evidence found in the book. At the moment, Winston wants to save his skin, so he carefully hides the diary.

SECTION III

Winston dreams he's with his mother in a sinking ship. We're reminded of the heroic refugee mother from the newsreel in Section I. Winston is struck with guilt. Although his mother disappeared in a political purge, he feels somehow responsible. We'll see why later.

In the next instant he is in a dream landscape in a place he calls The Golden Country, a stubbly pasture where the dark-haired girl appears. She strips naked and runs toward him. He sees this as an act of destruction—the girl wiping out the Party in one free gesture. (In a Party that suppresses sex, anything sexual is rebellion.) He wakes saying, "Shakespeare."

NOTE: Winston's Dreams

Look carefully at Winston's dreams. They're prophetic and symbolic. Every one signals something important to come in the book. Look at:

1. The dream about O'Brien. Yes, they are going to meet in the place where there is no darkness, but it's not what Winston thinks, as we find out in *Part Three*. He doesn't know the possible outcome but in his loneliness he can hardly wait.

2. The dream about his mother foreshadows memories to be revealed to Winston near the end of *Part Two*. Many people think Orwell uses the idea of woman as *mother* as ideal. What does this make of Julia, who has sex for fun? Watch how Orwell treats her and Winston's affair.

3. The Golden Country. This dream is the most heavily symbolic. It is directly prophetic, as you'll see when Winston finally meets the dark-haired girl; but there's more to it as an expression of Winston's yearning for the past. Look at:

   a. The country as England's rural past.
   b. The girl in her nakedness as a symbol of love, perhaps, but for Winston at this point, as rebellion.
   c. "Shakespeare." The arts in England have been wiped out by the Party. They, along with beauty and truth, are another part of the past that Winston longs for.

When he wakes, Winston reflects on childhood memories as he goes through the motions of his daily routine. Current history and his memories do not coincide. Oceania is and always was at war with Eurasia in alliance with Eastasia, according to all the books and papers, but this isn't the way Winston remembers it. The records are changed. "Doublethink" or "reality control" makes this possible: "To know and not to know . . . to hold simultaneously two opinions which canceled out, knowing them to be

contradictory and believing in both of them. . . . "
Revisionism, a political fact in some countries today, is
the ammunition of Orwell's imaginary Party.

NOTE: On Revisionism

Today we're familiar with revisionism—the altering of history texts and removal of certain images to
conform to prevailing policies. In some cases history is
revised because we have made new discoveries. For
instance, our wide knowledge of Franklin D. Roosevelt's illness has changed the way we look at his pres-
idency. While he was in office, the seriousness of his
illness was kept secret for the good of the government; the country was at war and needed to have
complete faith in the power of its president. In the
Soviet Union and the People's Republic of China, history has changed with the regimes. For instance, stat-
ues and pictures of Stalin, once prominent everywhere, have been removed from the Soviet Union, as
recent regimes have tried to disassociate themselves
from Stalin and his practices.

In Winston's case, a leader has been created. As he
remembers it, nobody had heard of Big Brother before
1960. Now that he's a figurehead, history has been
backdated so that there are tales of Big Brother's
exploits as far back as the 1930s. In Orwell's day, such
practices were relatively new. Since his death, history
has made his cautionary novel look like grim prophecy.

SECTION IV

Winston is at work in the Records section of the
Ministry of Truth, engaged in the kind of revision that
keeps the Party going. In his cubicle is a "speakwrite"

(today it would be a computer terminal); a tube for written messages and one for newspapers; and a "memory hole," in which he destroys obsolete documents. Today Winston would probably complete his entire operation on his handy word processor. As messages came up on the screen, he could note the necessary changes and record over them, erasing history with the touch of a button.

It's probably safe to guess that for Winston's feelings, at least, Orwell draws on his own World War II days with the BBC, when he wrote newscasts for broadcast in India. For morale purposes, then, certain facts would have to be withheld, and even defeats had to be described in an upbeat manner.

Winston's job is to update Big Brother's old speeches, in which the leader might have guessed wrong about where a skirmish with the enemy would take place, or how badly the chocolate ration is going to be cut. In the latter case Winston also has to make the cut in rations look like an increase. Later he's going to have to make this kind of change on a massive scale—watch for it.

Daily, Winston destroys the old documents and creates new ones to cover policy changes. All these changes have to be incorporated into new editions of back newspapers, books, and all written records; these are destroyed and replaced to keep up with "history." Could people really do this in Winston's day (Orwell's, rather), or even today? Perhaps Orwell was making his point by exaggeration.

Elsewhere in the Ministry of Truth, thousands of workers are creating cheap novels and daily horoscopes, all the trappings of the popular culture. The clever trash is designed to keep the proles so happy that they won't notice how many hardships and shortages the Party has caused. There is even a pornosec with a product so racy that Party members aren't allowed to peek. Remember this later when Winston reflects on the Party line on sex.

Today Winston is faced with a challenge. In Newspeak his order reads: "times e.12.83 reporting bb dayorder doubleplus ungood refs unpersons rewrite fullwise upsub antefiling." Orwell translates for us: "The reporting of Big Brother's Order for the Day in the *Times* of December 3rd 1983 is extremely unsatisfactory and makes references to nonexistent persons. Rewrite it in full and submit your draft to higher authority before filing."

The author is about to introduce a central concept. A former high Inner Party hero, praised in one of Big Brother's speeches, has mysteriously fallen out of favor and, we must guess, has been liquidated, or as Orwell has it, "vaporized." It is not enough that Big Brother has made him disappear. He must be expunged from the record. Not only does Comrade Withers cease to exist; he never did exist. Comrade Withers is now an *unperson*. This thinking is central to Party survival as we see in *Two, IX*, in Emmanuel Goldstein's book.

Winston revises the records brilliantly, by the simple expedient of invention.

Winston settles for a simple invention that calls for the fewest changes in records: he makes up Comrade Ogilvy. With tongue in cheek, Orwell, through Winston, presents a Party paragon who from infancy refuses all but military toys, turns in his uncle to the Thought Police at eleven, organizes the Junior Anti-Sex League, and at age seventeen designs a grenade that blows up thirty-one prisoners at one pop. He dies gallantly, and, according to this revised speech by Big Brother,

> He was a total abstainer and a non-smoker, had no recreations except a daily hour in the gymnasium, and had taken a vow of celibacy, believing marriage . . . to be incompatible with a twenty-four-hours-a-day devotion to duty. He had no subjects of conversation except the principles of Ingsoc, and no aim in life except the defeat of the Eurasian enemy and the hunting-down of spies, saboteurs, thought-criminals, and traitors generally.

Tickled with his invention, Winston decides not to award Comrade Ogilvy the Order of Conspicuous Merit because it will entail too many changes in the record.

NOTE: It's interesting at this point to look at two alterations in texts in the Soviet Union. In the course of World War II, the Soviets, who had been allied with Hitler, switched alliances to fight with England and the United States. *A Small Soviet Encyclopedia*, published in 1941, reflects a change in position that took place *in the middle of a press run.* Early copies describe U.S. President Roosevelt as a capitalist waging war for imperialist gain. By the end of the run, he has become the hope of the Russian people and a foe of fascism.

When the Russian leader Lavrenty Beria fell from favor he became an "unperson." Subscribers to the *Large Soviet Encyclopedia*, one scholar reports, were sent a set of fresh pages on the Bering Sea and entries on a little-known figure called Bergholz, to replace certain pages in the BER-section. They were to remove the Beria pages with a razor blade and insert the new ones. In 1952, Czechoslovak Communist Evan Loebl, accused of crimes against the state but not executed, underwent a long interrogation process that continued even after he had confessed. "I was quite a normal person," he said, "only I was not a person." Watch what happens to Winston later, in *Part Three*.

SECTION V

In the canteen, Winston lines up for lunch along with Syme, who works in the Research Department. Syme, a specialist in Newspeak, is preparing the Eleventh Edition of the Newspeak dictionary. He is tiny, sad, and too smart for his own good.

The food is vile, improved only slightly by the addition of Victory gin, the swill the Party provides, along with Victory Coffee and Victory Cigarettes, names echoing second-rate "Victory" products available in London after World War II, when conditions made it impossible for people to obtain anything better.

Winston prompts Syme to talk about the Eleventh Edition, which he does, saying gleefully that he is busy destroying thousands of words, along with the works of Shakespeare, Milton and others. This gives Orwell an opportunity to incorporate some of his political thinking into the text, although as a novelist he knows better than to drop it in whole. He dresses it up by pretending it's a dramatic conversation, weaving in Syme's manner and Winston's responses along with details about the setting. When he's finished, he still has a lot more to say hence the awkward *Appendix* elaborating on Newspeak.

Syme says, "Don't you see that the whole aim of Newspeak is to narrow the range of thought? In the end we shall make Thoughtcrime impossible because there will be no words in which to express it."

One of these days, Winston thinks, Syme is going to be vaporized. Syme points to a couple spouting Party jargon and introduces a new word: *duckspeak*. "Applied to an opponent, it is abuse; applied to someone you agree with, it is praise." He is clearly too intelligent and outgoing to survive in the Party.

In comes Parsons, a completely different kind of Party member. Pudgy and zealous, Parsons is collecting money for the neighborhood Hate Week; he can't wait to start decorating. He apologizes for his kids' harassing Winston, but he's clearly proud of their Party fervor.

All hands listen to a joyful announcement from the Ministry of Plenty that the chocolate ration has been raised—from thirty grams to twenty. How can people swallow this? It's either grin or be vaporized. It makes as much sense to Winston as the contrast between the ill-fed, funny-looking Party members and the Party ideal of handsome blonde stereotypes (not unlike Hitler's "ideal" Aryans).

Uncertain about how many of his rebellious thoughts show in his expression and gestures, Winston breaks into a sweat when he discovers he's being watched. The dark-haired girl whom he fears is a state spy sits at the next table.

SECTION VI

Winston records his last sexual encounter (with a prole prostitute) in his diary. The entry is a springboard for Orwell's consideration of sex and politics.

Being caught with a prostitute might get Winston five years in a labor camp, but the real crime is "promiscuity" between Party members, which at the moment Winston finds unthinkable because of his Party conditioning. He'd like it, but thinks nobody would dare.

The aim of the Party, Winston believes, is to remove all pleasure from sexual acts. Sex and marriage are a mere necessity, like "a slightly disgusting minor operation," to be undertaken for the purpose of producing infant Party members. He understands that the Party is trying to suppress the sexual instinct—but for purposes he hasn't yet identified.

His ex-wife Katharine had a "stupid, vulgar, empty" mind and shrank from sex, submitting only for Party purposes. When it became clear that she and Winston were not going to produce a baby, they separated.

Orwell has political reasons for drawing women and sex the way he does in this chapter. He also has artistic reasons: to show us that Winston is lonely and ready for the affair with Julia. He also wants us to know that Winston has more than love in mind:

"And what he wanted, more even than to be loved, was to break down that wall of virtue, even if it were only once in his whole life." This is romantic, but look at what he thinks next: "The sexual act, successfully performed, was rebellion."

Does Winston think of women as something to be used, or is this Orwell's view? Watch the unfolding affair with Julia and decide whether you think Winston is ever really in love with her. Does he respect Julia for who she is, or is she simply the first available woman?

Back to the diary. Winston's remembered prostitute took him to her room where he discovered that she was old, ugly, and made him feel dirty. He took her anyway.

SECTION VII

Winston writes: "If there is hope it is in the *proles*." The proles, Winston thinks, could shake off the Party as a horse shakes off flies— if they could be roused. But his example of their potential for rebellion is a few hundred prole women stampeding for a bunch of tin saucepans. Two bloated women tug over a pan; their quarreling disgusts him:

> Left to themselves, like cattle . . . they had reverted to . . . a sort of ancestral pattern. They were born, they grew up in the gutters, they went to work at twelve, they passed through a brief blossoming period of beauty and sexual desire, they married at twenty, they were middle-aged at thirty, they died, for the most part, at sixty.

This seems to be the best they can do. It isn't much! Their minds are so simple that the Thought Police can keep them in line. Being without general ideas, they can only focus their discontent on petty grievances. They watch football or have sex at will because, as a Party slogan sums it up: "Proles and animals are free."

Is this really what Winston thinks about the common people? Is it what Orwell thinks? If it is—and we never know for certain—both character and author are dreadful pessimists, and Winston's later reflection that the *proles* are the hope for the future is an empty one.

Remember that in describing the Ministry of Truth Orwell exaggerates to get our attention. He may be exaggerating here in order to underscore his warning to his fellow Englishmen, and to make them so mad at him that they will wake up and take action. Perhaps his response to the proles is so conditioned by his years at St. Cyprian's, Eton and Burma that he has let his ingrained sense of the British class system and his snobbery get the better of him. See what you think.

NOTE: Some readers think the fact that Orwell was dying while he finished this novel accounts for the pessimistic view of society and its future, while others think he was using every weapon in his arsenal to wake up his readers. Remember, only a few years earlier Hitler tried to create a world similar to *1984* in Germany, and Russia was in the grip of a strong centralized government at the time that Orwell was writing.

Picking up a revised children's history, Winston tries to sort out the truths from the lies. Was London really worse off before the Revolution? The Party claims to build ideal cities, but Winston's London is a shambles. He has trouble remembering the past because "Everything faded into mist. The past was erased, the erasure was forgotten, the lie became truth."

Just once in his life, Winston possessed concrete evidence of a Party lie. It happened this way: In the Middle Sixties, the original leaders of the Revolution were wiped out. Among the last arrested were Jones, Aaronson, and Rutherford, who disappeared and then came back to make public confessions. They were pardoned and reinstated. Winston once saw them in the Chestnut Tree Cafe, a questionable hangout for discredited Party members, where a song played: "Under the spreading chestnut tree I sold you and you sold me. . . ." As Winston watched, Rutherford heard the song and began to weep. We'll see the cafe and hear the song again in Part Three. Several years later Winston comes upon a photograph that proved the "traitors" were really in New York when they were supposed to be in Eurasia, committing crimes against the state. (This paralleled a similar case in the Soviet Union during Orwell's lifetime.) Winston held in his hand physical proof—the photograph—that the Party had lied. Frightened, he destroyed it, but he still remembers. "The past not only changed, but changed continuously." He writes in his diary: *I understand HOW: I do not understand WHY.*

Winston may very well be the only man alive who remembers or cares about the truth.

In the last section Orwell prepared us for Winston's encounter with Julia. In this section he prepares us for Winston's confrontation with the Party. Note that Winston looks to a woman to express his rebellion. In his loneliness, he also turns to O'Brien. He is writing the diary for—or to—O'Brien. Pay close attention to the last thing Winston writes: "Freedom is the freedom to say that two plus two make four. If that is granted, all else follows." Orwell is setting him up for his destruction, as we see in Part Three.

SECTION VIII

It's a nice evening and although solitary acts are frowned on, Winston goes for a walk. He is drawn to the *prole* sector, where a shouted warning flattens him just as a rocket bomb (like the "buzz bombs" of World War II) hits. Winston thinks proles have some instinct that lets them know about such things.

As he wanders among them, he sees the common people as sexual, careless, almost animal in their simple pleasures, which include the Lottery and drinking in pubs. He envies their simplicity, a fact which some readers would argue is a figment of the author's class-conscious imagination. Others say he is exaggerating for effect. What do you think?

In the pub, Winston fastens on an old man as a possible link to the past. Certainly the man remembers the days before Big Brother. But when they try to talk, the man seems to remember only gents in top hats who wanted him to touch his cap, and times when he wasn't plagued by a twitchy bladder. What Winston is trying to find out is whether the Party line is true: that the lower classes were oppressed by bloated capitalists in the terrible days of hardship that were ended by the Revolution, when the Party came to power.

"Was life better before the Revolution than it is now?" Winston knows the question is not answerable because all the relevant facts are outside the range of vision of the old people who might remember. When memory fails and the records are altered, there is no standard against which the Party's claims can be tested. Orwell seems to foresee a time in which the elite will be at work altering the records, leaving the past to the apparently faulty memories of the lower classes.

Winston retreats to the streets and discovers that the secondhand shop where he bought the diary is still open. Mr. Charrington, the white-haired proprietor, smiles kindly and welcomes Winston. The gold and silver of yesteryear have been melted down, so what remains in his shop has little tangible value, except as a link with the past that Winston has been seeking.

On a table in the back is a rounded glass paperweight. Except for the image of Big Brother on posters and telescreens, it is the single most important object in the shop. The glass is clear as rainwater, and at its center is a lovely pink shape. The paperweight is important to Winston as a symbol of the lost past. It has another equally important symbolic role in the story, which we'll discover in Part Two. The old man tells Winston that the pink shape is coral, and, as soon as Winston buys it, offers to show him his private upstairs room. It is here that Winston will play some of his most important scenes as the novel unfolds.

The room itself is an emblem of more civil times, when a man could sit by the fire with his feet up, safe from the watchful television eye. Ah, the old man says, he never had the money for the telescreen, and never felt the need of it. He owns only a few worthless books—everything printed before 1960 has been destroyed by the Party.

The room does, however, contain one other major item: a print of St. Clement's Dane, one of London's most venerable churches. The frame, the old man says, is fixed to the wall. Keep an eye on this print; it's important for several reasons:

1. It's a symbol of London's lost past, which Winston longs for. The church has been half-destroyed and turned to other uses by the Party.

2. It's a springboard for the children's rhyme that is repeated throughout the novel: "Oranges and lemons, say the bells of St. Clement's; you owe me three farthings, say the bells of St. Martin's. . . ." The rhyme moves Winston as he reflects on the fate of London's churches.

3. Like Mr. Charrington, the print is not what it seems—as we'll discover at the end of Part Two.

Leaving Mr. Charrington reluctantly, Winston heads home with the paperweight in his pocket. His heart almost stops when he sees a figure in blue overalls. It's the dark-haired girl, and he fears she is following him. Paralyzed, he wonders if he can brain her with the incriminating paperweight. He heads home, frightened and drained of the will to resist.

He takes out his diary, reflecting: "It was at night that they came for you, always at night. The proper thing was to kill yourself before they got to you." In what he took to be a moment of danger with the girl, Winston had lost the power to act.

This section is important to any study of Winston's character, since he thinks about O'Brien and about what will happen to him after the Thought Police take him away. He knows that before death he will suffer torture, but wonders why: after all, nobody ever escaped detection or failed to confess. "Why then, did that horror, which altered nothing, have to lie embedded in future time?"

He reflects again on what he thinks O'Brien said: "We shall meet in the place where there is no darkness." He thinks he knows where this is. It's the "imagined future, which one would never see, but which, by foreknowledge, one could mystically share in." Is this Winston's death wish at work? His loneliness? His desire to be like other people? It may be all three.

From a coin, Big Brother stares at him. He studies the legend:

WAR IS PEACE
FREEDOM IS SLAVERY
IGNORANCE IS STRENGTH

NOTE: Orwell never quite manages to explain these slogans in the course of the novel, so they are defined in an unwieldly extract from Emmanuel Goldstein's revolutionary bible. We'll discuss this when we get to Part Two.

PART TWO

SECTION I

It's morning. Winston is heading for the men's room when he sees the dark-haired girl who frightened him so the other night. She's wearing a sling and falls on her injured arm. Winston helps her up. To his astonishment, she slips him a note which, after elaborate precautions, he reads and destroys. In her unformed handwriting she has written:

I love you.

He wants a few minutes alone to consider this, but Parsons joins him, babbling about decorations for Hate Week. All afternoon he is haunted by the girl's face. At the sight of the words *I love you*, "the desire to stay alive had welled up in him, and the taking of minor risks suddenly seemed stupid." He goes through the motions of the business day, hiding what he feels.

How are he and the girl going to meet without raising suspicions? Maybe he can bump into her in the canteen. The next week is one of fevered anticipation and worry. Finally they manage to sit at the same lunch table, speaking without looking up so anyone watching won't see.

They meet in Victory Square under the eyes of several telescreens, but crowd movement allows them to slip close and make plans as truckloads of Eurasian prisoners go by. They will take separate trains out of Paddington station and meet on a country lane Julia knows. For a second they hold hands.

SECTION II

Winston is in the country, perhaps for the first time since childhood. Has he spent his adult life in the city because it suits the author's convenience or are there other reasons? See what you think.

The couple meet in a flowered field, free from hidden microphones. Here they can escape the drabness, the crowded conditions, the sameness of city life. The girl, whom Winston thinks of as "experienced," has been here before. They exchange a few words and then embrace. She is young and attractive, but when she kisses him he feels not desire, only disbelief and pride.

Her name is Julia, she says. He tells her his name and confesses that he almost bashed her with the paperweight because he thought she worked for the Thought Police. She rips off the Junior Anti-Sex League sash and hands him a piece of chocolate. He can't understand why she is attracted to him, as he's older.

"It was something in your face," she says. ". . . As soon as I saw you I knew you were against *them*."

Julia leads Winston to a secret woods, where he remembers at once the "Golden Country" of his dreams. Orwell now gives us a loving description of the country, and of a singing bird. Winston's desire awakens. When he and Julia come together the experience is almost as lovely as it was in his dream in *Part One*.

Has Julia done this before? Yes, she says, with

scores of Party members. Winston is not distressed; on the contrary, "he wished it had been hundreds— thousands. Anything that hinted at corruption filled him with a wild hope. . . . Anything to rot, to weaken, to undermine!" Since Winston equates sex with rebellion, he tells her that the more men she has had, the more he loves her. She says she loves sex and is "corrupt to the bone," and they embrace. It is not Julia alone that arouses him but rebellion, "not merely the love of one person, but the animal instinct, the simple undifferentiated desire: that was the force that would tear the Party to pieces."

Rebellion is what flames Winston's desire. He realizes rolling away from her, that there is no pure love and no pure lust in a world ruled by the Party, since everything is polluted with fear and hatred. If we are to believe Winston, his response to Julia is the Party's fault.

SECTION III

When Julia wakes she is all business, dealing with the details of their safe return home. It is clear that she has a "practical cunning" which Winston lacks. Unlike Winston, Julia is open and breezy. She flings her arms around him and then leaves. They go home by separate routes, with plans for a future rendezvous.

They never go back to the clearing in the fields. The next time, they meet in another of her hiding places, a ruined church in a countryside leveled by an atomic bomb. Their other meetings are rushed encounters in which they exchange a few words. The logistics of work hours and Party activities (if you keep the small rules, says Julia, you can break the big ones) keep them apart most of the time.

At the church, Julia describes her life in a hostel

with thirty other girls ("Always the stink of women! How I hate women!") She says she is "not clever," but she feels at home with the machinery that composes novels in the Fiction Department where she works. Because Julia is young, *her memories are Party memories.* All the workers in the Pornosec are girls because they're supposed to be "so pure" that they won't be aroused by the material. She knows that she herself is no longer "pure" enough.

Julia describes her first affair and gives her view of life. Her rebellion against the Party consists in having a good time without the Party's finding out. She has no interest in Party doctrine, has never heard of the secret Brotherhood and thinks organized rebellion against the party is stupid. The clever thing is to break all the rules and stay alive.

Julia gives us a good overview of why the Party Prohibits sex. The Party's sexual repressiveness, she says, is designed to induce hysteria that can be turned into war fever and leader worship. Making love uses up energy that could be turned to Party ends. Privation creates hostility that can be turned on the Party's enemies. The Family has been turned into an extension of the Thought Police—everybody is surrounded by informants. (It *takes Julia to point this out to Winston; she is the clever one.*)

Winston recalls a hike (perhaps his only other excursion to the country) with his wife Katharine. When he showed her some flowers on the side of a cliff, he thought of pushing her off. He didn't have the nerve, though, and he didn't believe it would matter whether he pushed her or not, since "In this game that we're playing, we can't win." Winston seems to be a defeatist, who knows things will end badly. Julia's function is to deny that they are doomed, to insist on the power of luck and cunning and boldness. To Winston's "We are the dead," Julia replies, "We're not dead yet."

Orwell seems to use the couple as speakers for opposite sides of an argument. Either the world is so far gone that there is no hope, no matter how hard people struggle, or people are strong and resourceful and there is hope. People either can't change their circumstances—or they can. In this novel Orwell seems to load the dice against his characters, but in this part of the story, at least, there appears to be some reason for the characters—and the reader—to hope.

SECTION IV

Winston has taken a drastic step. He has rented the room above Mr. Charrington's shop so he and Julia will have a place to be alone together. On the gateleg table in the corner is the glass paperweight. In fact, a vision of the paperweight on Mr. Charrington's table is what inspired him to risk capture by renting the room.

Outside, somebody is singing. It is "a monstrous woman, solid as a pillar, with brawny red forearms." She is hanging up diapers and singing aloud, something no Party member would ever do. Keep an eye on this woman, as she is central to Winston's story and carries one conscious message from the author as well as—perhaps—an unconscious one. We'll come to her later.

Overworked as the city prepares for Hate Week, Winston and Julia have had to put off meeting because she is having her period. He is surprised now by how angry this makes him. Their first act of love was, for him, an intellectual gesture, but now he finds he wants and needs her, and wishes they had the leisure to be like an old married couple, walking out together, able to be alone together "without feeling the obligation to make love every time they met." It is for this reason that he has rented the room.

This section portrays Winston as much more of a romantic lover than he seemed in his first encounter with Julia, but he is still a fatalist, thinking: "It was as though they were intentionally stepping nearer to their graves." This seems to make something of a star-crossed lover of him; in other words he is in love precisely because the love is doomed.

Julia enters, with packets of sugar, real coffee, and real bread, luxury items usually reserved for Inner Party members. She has brought something else. She tells him to turn his back. Once again he sees the red-armed woman in the courtyard and thinks she would be happy to go on like that forever, singing and hanging up the wash.

When he turns around, he's delighted because Julia has put on makeup. He has never seen a Party woman with a painted face. She looks not only prettier, but "far more feminine." But when he takes her in his arms, he notices that she's wearing the same perfume as his last prostitute.

Most of Winston's thoughts, however, are romantic. He lets Julia see him naked for the first time. They sleep in the double bed as light from the sunset slants into the room, and, waking, Winston wonders whether in the old days couples always had the leisure to dawdle in bed after making love.

His reverie is shattered by the appearance of a rat. Winston shudders with horror because he is assailed by memories of a recurring nightmare. In his dream, he is standing in front of a wall of darkness, looking out on something too dreadful to be faced. It has something to do with rats, he thinks. Remember the dream. It's important in Part Three.

Julia reassures him and then gets up to tour the room, investigating the shabby antiques with some amusement, and bringing the paperweight back to the bed. Winston calls the paperweight a "little chunk of history that they've forgotten to alter. It's a message from a hundred years ago. . . ." When she looks at the picture of St. Clement's, Winston recites the first two lines of the old verse and Julia fills in the next two: "You owe me three farthings, say the bells of St. Martin's, When will you pay me? say the bells of Old Bailey. . . ."

Julia may not know the next two lines but she remembers the end: "Here comes a candle to light you to bed, here comes a chopper to chop off your head!"

After Julia leaves, Winston gazes into the glass paperweight. He imagines the glass as the arch of the sky, a whole world containing himself and this room full of antiques: "The paperweight was the room he was in, and the coral was Julia's life and his own, fixed in a sort of eternity at the heart of the crystal."

NOTE: Here, as elsewhere in *1984*, Orwell uses objects—an antique table, an antique clock, a print of the church of St. Clement's Dane—to create atmosphere and to give the reader a strong sense of place. Through Winston's response to these objects, we get a clear picture of Winston's love for the past. All novelists use details to bring us into rooms we've never seen; many, like Orwell, use physical objects to stand

for much more than their face value. The paperweight, as we saw after Julia left, a symbol of the past.
Keep an eye on that picture of the church, which Julia
offered to take down and clean. It also reminds Winston of the past, and of the old verse, but it has one
last function to perform.

SECTION V

Syme has become an *unperson;* it happened overnight. In the summer heat, with the city wheels grind-
ing around the clock in preparation for Hate Week,
Winston hardly notices. Proles and the Parsons children alike are singing and playing a new ditty
drummed up for the occasion, "Hate Song." The
senior Parsons is hanging banners and streamers in
the heat, in preparation for the event.

Even the proles are fired up, by the weather, by an
increase in flights of rocket bombs, and by a huge
poster of a Eurasian soldier that appears everywhere,
inspiring hate. Winston retreats with Julia to the room
above Mr. Charrington's—the two lovers are swelter-
ing and pestered by bugs, but content.

The affair has been good for Winston, who has
given up gin and begun to put on a little weight. He's
cheered by the knowledge that the room is available,
even when he can't get to it. The room to him is a
world, a pocket of the past, where extinct animals can
talk." Everything he cares about is here.

One of Winston's extinct animals is Mr. Charrington, who produces memories in the same way that he
produces antiques to charm Winston.

In this section we see Winston and Julia as star-
crossed lovers once more. Even Julia knows their hap-

piness can't last long and this inspires them to "despairing sensuality," which makes the affair seem sweeter. Until now, you could have argued that Winston was a sexist who used Julia as a weapon in his private revolution. But during this interlude he gives signals that his love has come to mean more.

Winston begins to have fantasies: that their affair can last; that he can escape with Julia into the world of the paperweight, where time stops; that Katharine will die so they can marry; that they can commit suicide; that they can change their identities and live among the proles.

"In reality"—writes Orwell—"there was no escape." Why not? Julia knew her way around—why couldn't she and Winston disappear from view and live a happy life among the proles? There was no reason why Orwell couldn't have arranged for them to be caught, later in order to satisfy the purpose of his novel.

There are two possible reasons why the lovers don't try to escape:

1.   By the time Orwell finished his first draft of the novel and began a second one, he was ailing. Perhaps he lacked the physical strength to add additional chapters to his book.

2.   Perhaps Orwell, like Winston, was a slave to his class. Even when the author was living among the coal miners and their families, he was not one of them. He was revolted by unpleasant sights and smells. Neither he nor Winston would be comfortable living among such people; it would have been out of the question.

Instead of plotting their escape, Winston and Julia begin to talk about rebellion—finding their way into the secret Brotherhood. He tells her about the "strange intimacy" he feels with the sophisticated Inner Party member O'Brien, even though they have never met.

We begin to hear about Julia's political attitudes. She can't believe that there will ever be widespread opposition to the Party. She assumes, however, that everybody like herself, rebels privately. She believes that stories about Emmanuel Goldstein and the war in Eurasia are Party inventions designed to keep people in line.

Although Julia believes in love, she knows that the Party is an unalterable fact of life and that "You could only rebel against it by secret disobedience or, at most, by isolated acts of violence such as killing somebody or blowing something up." Her own particular rebellion is sexual.

It's Julia who suggests that the government has invented the war and arranges for the rocket bomb to fall to keep everybody on their toes. At the same time she buys the Party myths "because the difference between truth and falsehood did not seem important to her."

Is she a featherbrain or a realist? Orwell and Winston seem to want to see her both ways. Julia makes some profound observations about politics, yet when Winston tells her about the picture he saw of Jones, Aaronson and Rutherford and how it proved the Party lied, she is indifferent, telling him: "I'm not interested in the next generation, dear. I'm interested in *us*." And when he calls her "a rebel from the waist downwards," she hugs him in wild delight.

Do Winston and his creator respect this woman? In some lights, yes. In some, no. They admire her cheerful realism, may even envy it, but Winston undercuts this by thinking: "In a way, the world-view of the Party imposed itself most successfully on people incapable of understanding it. . . . By lack of understanding they remained sane."

SECTION VI

Just when Winston begins to think that Julia isn't a fit intellectual companion, O'Brien gets in touch. Winston thinks this is what he's been waiting for all his life.

Meeting O'Brien in the halls of the Ministry, Winston is speechless. His heart pounds. Is he merely excited at being in the presence of an important political figure, or is his attraction more personal and profound? Defining the nature of this attraction is going to help us decide what Winston's feelings for O'Brien really are.

At the moment he is thrilled because O'Brien praises his work and alludes to the missing Syme—a hint that O'Brien may be a Party enemy, too. O'Brien offers to show him a Newspeak dictionary if he'll drop by one evening after work. He gives Winston his address. Winston is sure he's reached the outer edges of the Brotherhood.

Winston sees this as the next step in a process that, for him, began years ago. The first step was a secret thought. The second was the diary. The third, we can assume, was his affair with Julia. The next will be his relationship with O'Brien, and after that?

"The last step was something that would happen in the Ministry of Love. . . . The end was contained in the beginning. . . . He had always known that the grave was there and waiting for him." These sound like the thoughts of a man who is in love not with Julia, not with O'Brien, but with death.

NOTE: One critic has raised the possibility that *1984* is not a political novel at all, but an existential one. If we remember that Winston is "The Last (thinking) Man in Europe," we can recognize the truth in this. The Party and the unwashed proles alike underscore Winston's isolation both in thought and body; and the fact that he never really finds a kindred soul guarantees his despair. His girlfriend doesn't understand him and his mentor, O'Brien, seeks to destroy him. If we accept this interpretation, then *1984* is the story of one man's intellectual and actual loneliness, and his "rebellion" is, rather, a planned suicide. In this interpretation O'Brien is quite simply, the means to death, which Winston embraces as he would a lover.

This is an unorthodox interpretation, but one you may have fun playing with since Winston marches straight into the clutches of O'Brien and the power he represents.

SECTION VII

Winston wakes from another dream. This one does not so much foreshadow future events as trigger a memory. His dream takes place inside the paperweight, which Orwell gave us as an emblem for the past. In the dream he discovers that the arm gesture made by the refugee mother in the newsreel is one his mother made.

Until this moment, he tells Julia, he had believed that he caused his mother's death.

He recalls a childhood spent hiding out in Underground stations during air raids. His father was already gone and the city was a shambles. His mother is dead at heart. They are hungry all the time. He remembers badgering his mother for food; he takes food from her and his baby sister because hunger is the strongest thing he feels. In one last guilty act he steals chocolate from both of them, and runs away.

He tells Julia he never saw them again. She mumbles, "All children are swine," and drifts off to sleep. Winston remembers his mother protecting his baby sister, and thinks: "The terrible thing that the Party had done was to persuade you that mere impulses, mere feelings, were of no account. . . ." He admires his mother for making the protective gesture *in spite of the fact* that she knows her family is doomed.

The proles, he thinks, still harbor such emotions. They are human, whereas Party members have their emotions suppressed. "We are not human," he says.

Julia is awake now, and they agree that the best and safest thing would be to separate and never come here again. Yet they both seem to belong to a past in which emotions mattered, and they know they can't and won't separate.

They talk about the loneliness of capture. Julia points out that yes, they will confess, but nothing can make her stop loving him. Winston hopes he will feel the same way. "They can't get inside you," he says. "If you can *feel* that staying human is worth while, even when it can't have any result whatever, you've beaten them." Orwell will show us the irony of these brave speeches in Part Three.

Just when human commitment seems possible, Orwell propels his brave couple into a rash gesture that leaves us crying out, Be careful!

This is, essentially, the couple's last chance to proceed cautiously, their last opportunity to change course, flee or seek out another hiding place. What do they do instead? They throw caution to the wind and take a fatal step forward.

SECTION VIII

If only there were some way we could warn Winston! But he is too full of hope and confidence. "They had done it," he says, "they had done it at last!"

They've gone to O'Brien's house. We've seen enough spy movies to know that you go to such meetings separately, and in disguise. Not these two. With almost nothing to go on, except an equivocal glance, Winston has brought the woman he loves to the command post of the Brotherhood.

First, let's look around O'Brien's apartment, another place where Orwell uses detail to put us in the picture and to tell us about the characters.

Winston is impressed. A servant has shown them into a softly lit room with a velvety carpet. It's a far cry from the squalor of Victory Mansions and the shabby room above Charrington's shop. They smell good food and real tobacco; they are intimidated by the Asian servant in the white coat. Everything is exquisitely clean. Although he is a self-styled writer of the people, Orwell seems to love to dwell on these upper-class luxuries.

O'Brien is at his desk. He delivers a final message to the speakwrite and turns off his telescreen. Winston is astonished. "You can turn it off!"

This is a privilege.

At the glimmer of a smile from O'Brien, Winston declares himself. In fact, he declares both of them. He and Julia are enemies of the Party, he says, thoughtcriminals and adulterers who want to join the Brotherhood. He is saying this so they will be at O'Brien's mercy; he wants to make it clear that they are trustworthy.

As he finishes speaking, the servant enters. O'Brien

tells Winston not to worry, the servant is "one of us."
O'Brien pours them glasses of wine, a rarity in the
days of Victory gin. They drink to Emmanuel Goldstein, who, O'Brien tells them, is a real person, not a
Party fabrication. According to O'Brien, Goldstein is
still alive and the Brotherhood is a reality.

O'Brien tells Winston something he should have
been smart enough to know (unless, as some readers
suspect, Winston has a death wish): that it was dangerous for the couple to come together. They have to
leave separately, Julia first.

Ignoring Julia, taking it for granted that Winston
speaks for both of them, O'Brien leads Winston
through a strange litany that almost echoes Christian
baptismal ceremonies. They agree to give their lives,
commit murder, commit numerous alien acts on behalf of the Brotherhood, to commit suicide, to part
forever. . . . "No!" the lovers cry, and O'Brien praises
them for telling him how they truly feel.

Dismissing the servant, O'Brien offers quality cigarettes and tells the couple they will be working in the
dark, obeying orders without knowing why. They'll
never know who the others in the Brotherhood are.

Winston is transfixed by O'Brien's authority, his
natural grace: "When you looked at O'Brien's powerful shoulders and his blunt-featured face, so ugly and
yet so civilized, it was impossible to believe that he
could be defeated." Even Julia is impressed.

The success of the organization, O'Brien says, de-
pends on secrecy. After they drink to the past (Winston's choice), O'Brien dismisses Julia.

In exchange for Winston's disclosure of his secret
hiding place, O'Brien offers to send him a copy of the
bible of the Brotherhood, rebel leader Emmanuel
Goldstein's book. Winston will regret this the day he

finds his briefcase exchanged for an identical one carrying the book.

Perhaps we will meet again, says O'Brien; and Winston answers at once, "In the place where there is no darkness?" Without surprise, O'Brien echoes the phrase. This has been so carefully prepared by the author that it hits with a satisfying thump.

At Winston's instigation O'Brien supplies the missing line to the "Oranges and lemons" rhyme. The second line is, "When will you pay me? say the bells of Old Bailey," to which O'Brien adds, "When I grow rich, say the bells of Shoreditch." This calls to mind the telling last line: "Here comes the chopper to chop off your head." Winston remembers this line but he has chosen to suppress it.

SECTION IX

It is in this section that art and politics collide and Orwell's fascination with his message gets in the way of the story. It contains great huge swatches of the Goldstein book, which echoes political writings of the time, including *The Managerial Revolution* and *The Machiavellians*, both by James Burnham; *The Revolution Betrayed*, by Leon Trotsky, and perhaps *Das Kapital*, by Karl Marx.

Unfortunately, for readers of fiction, political theory is never as gripping as the question of what's going to happen to the characters, which is why this chapter almost breaks the back of the book. Fortunately, Orwell is a good enough writer to keep us going. He has raised enough questions about the fate of Winston and Julia to make us sit still for this ideological interruption. We may squirm a little, but when the lights come up on the show after the political interlude, we're still in our seats.

Winston is "gelatinous" with fatigue after putting in a ninety-hour week. Right in the middle of Hate Week, history took an abrupt about-face and Oceania was *not* at war with Eurasia at all. Oceania was at war with Eastasia; Oceania and Eurasia were fighting side by side.

You can imagine how much alteration of records this involved, including quick changes in the middle of one Inner Party member's speech. As the people listen to this "little Rumpelstiltskin figure, contorted with hatred," they realize that the enemy has changed and that they're carrying the wrong signs! Orwell is clearly exaggerating for comic effect, showing us how arbitrary these changes are, and how easily the people are manipulated. Hate Week goes on.

Winston is anxious to do as good a job as he can because he's conscientious about his work; he's even proud of a good job well done. But he's also the secret rebel who is disgusted by outrageous doublethink of this kind. He is, furthermore, carrying Goldstein's book.

After work, Winston retreats to the room at Mr. Charrington's, where he leafs through the book and waits for Julia to arrive. He's thrilled to be reading The Book, called

The Theory and Practice
of Oligarchical Collectivism
by Emmanuel Goldstein.

This is Orwell's chance to talk ideology with us. Let's study the major points.

Chapter 1
IGNORANCE IS STRENGTH

The opening section divides the world into three orders of people: High, Middle and Low. They've always been divided; they've always had opposing and irreconcilable aims. The names have changed over the centuries but "the essential structure of society has never altered."

Orwell is going to have Winston skip to another chapter and then return to this one. He spells out the class divisions here so that he can go on to Goldstein's discussion of the High order (in Oceania, called the Inner Party), or hierarchy, with this eternal division established. In *1984*, O'Brien, the privileged, sophisticated Inner Party member, represents this High order. The Middle order includes Winston and Julia and the various bit players (minor characters) like Syme, Parsons, and Winston's other colleagues at work. This group takes orders from the High order and has to scrape along without the High order's luxuries or authority; yet it's still better off (according to Goldstein) than the Low order. Naturally the Low order in *1984* is made up of our friends the proles.

Orwell is clearly exaggerating to make his point, but you may want to remember that Orwell was the poor boy in a rich man's school, which must have formed his ideas on the High order. In his "down and out" days he went among the lower class as a kind of sightseer. He was not one of them; he only wrote about them. This may account for his portrayal of the *proles* as more or less mindless masses ill-equipped to rebel.

As Orwell lets Winston skip to Goldstein's Chapter 3, remember:

1.   The book is drawn from many real-life sources, including the ones named at the head of this section in your guide.

2. Orwell is drawing both on his knowledge of Communism in Stalin's Russia, and his memories of Hitler's Germany.

3. As he was writing, in the years after World War II, the U.S. and Great Britain were already allied. The Soviet Union was beginning to consolidate its power in Eastern European countries. The phrase "Cold War" had entered the language. British leader Winston Churchill had described the division between Eastern and Western European countries as the "Iron Curtain."

4. Orwell is using Goldstein's analysis to underscore his warning against allowing any government to gain too much power.

Since Goldstein repeats himself, it's useful to look at his argument point by point, as Orwell spells it out.

Chapter 3

WAR IS PEACE

Goldstein describes a world in which Russia has absorbed all of Europe to make Eurasia. The U.S. has absorbed the British Empire to form Oceania. Eastasia has emerged as the third power after decades of fighting. It is made up of China and countries to the south, Japan, and "a large but fluctuating portion of Manchuria, Mongolia and Tibet." These three superpowers are permanently at war, but it is a strictly limited, frontier war conducted by a small number of specialists, either at sea, around Floating Fortresses, or "on the vague frontiers whose whereabouts the ordinary man can only guess at." These boundaries keep changing as each side enjoys a temporary victory.

Reading any current issue of a newspaper or news

magazine, you'll be surprised at how many news stories recreate this very same scenario. None of the three superpowers, Goldstein says, can be totally conquered, even by the other two in combination. They're too evenly matched, and protected by their geography and resources. Between their frontiers are stretches of territory that keep changing hands: equatorial Africa, certain Middle Eastern countries, Southern India and Indonesia, which are rich in resources and heavily populated, providing "a bottomless reserve of cheap labor." The fighting flows back and forth in these areas.

"The primary aim of modern warfare [in accordance with the principles of *doublethink*, this aim is simultaneously recognized and not recognized by the directing brains of the Inner Party] is to use up the products of the machine without raising the general standard of living." Why is this so?

According to Goldstein, the opening of the machine age in the early 1900s should have ended human drudgery and therefore created human equality. In a world where everybody had enough to eat and a comfortable place to live, inequality would disappear and wealth would confer no distinction. What would happen to power them? A literate society would sweep it away.

To protect itself, the High order mentioned in Goldstein's first chapter had to keep the masses in poverty and ignorance. The most efficient way to do this was to wage war. "The essential act of war is destruction, not necessarily of human lives, but of the products of human labor," Goldstein says.

The war effort engages people and resources that might otherwise be directed toward making life too comfortable for the masses. War:

1. Eats up any surplus. This means luxury goods are reserved for the Inner Party, a fact that underscores the high position of the High order. The few goods that filter down to Outer Party members separate them from the *proles*. The hierarchy is enforced.

2. Encourages the people to hand authority over to a hierarchy. "The consciousness of being at war, and therefore in danger, makes the handing-over of all power to a small caste seem the natural, unavoidable condition of survival."

The Party fosters a wartime mentality. This means fear of the enemy (whomever the enemy is at any given time); hatred of the enemy; love for the Party, and the joy of triumph at Party victories.

According to Goldstein this wartime mentality is strongest in Inner Party members. Although these members may know that certain news is false, or that there is no real war, through *doublethink* they believe in the war anyway, even as they believe in victory when no real victory is possible.

To keep this system in operation, the Party turns to technology to refine methods of thought control and to develop new ways to kill great numbers of people efficiently, because "The two aims of the Party are to conquer the whole surface of the earth and to extinguish once and for all the possibility of independent thought."

It is amazing to Goldstein that the world remains unchanged, even though all three superpowers have the atomic bomb (it first exploded in 1945, two years before Orwell began this book). The powers have concluded that dropping the bomb would spell the end to organized society and therefore to their power. We don't have to look beyond U.S.-Soviet SALT (Strategic

Arms Limitation Treaty) negotiations to find modern parallels.

None of the superstates will invade any of the others because:

1. They won't risk a step that might cause serious defeat.

2. "Cultural integrity" must be maintained. Oceania, for example, must keep its people ignorant of other societies. If the average citizen met the "enemy,"

    a. He'd find out the "enemy" is very like himself, and "The fear, hatred, and self-righteousness on which his morale depends might evaporate."

    b. He'd find conditions in all three superstates are much the same, and therefore learn that there would be no advantage to victory and no point to war.

    c. He'd find that all three ruling philosophies are much alike and that the systems they support are basically the same, with the same structure, the same worship of a semi-divine leader, the same economy existing by and for continuous warfare.

Remaining in conflict, the three powers prop one another up. With no real danger of conquest, they can deny reality. In the old days, Goldstein writes, "Physical facts could not be ignored. In philosophy, or religion, or ethics, or politics, two and two make five, but when one was designing a gun or an airplane they had to make four." Efficient rulers learned from past mistakes, so they needed a knowledge of history. Confronting real risks, their goals were checked by reality.

With a continuous war in which there is no real

danger, the citizen's grip on reality is determined by what the Party tells him. He's like "a man in interstellar space, who has no way of knowing which direction is up and which is down." Continuous war preserves the special mental atmosphere which a hierarchical society needs, for the Higher order to maintain power.

This is an important point because it's one of the underpinnings of Party philosophy in the novel. It certainly helps explain why O'Brien, in *Part Three*, tries to hammer into Winston's head that "two and two equals five"—a formula that Orwell uses to stand for all the other mental acts of surrender a Party victim must make.

Goldstein writes: "The war is waged by each ruling group against its own subjects, and the object of the war is not to make or prevent conquests of territory, but to keep the structure of society intact." By becoming continuous, war has ceased to exist. The effect would be similar if the three superstates agreed to live in peaceful isolation, each "a self-contained universe, freed forever from the sobering influence of external danger." This is the inner meaning of:

WAR IS PEACE

At this point Orwell must have realized he was taxing his readers with too much theory, and so he has Julia come in and throw herself into Winston's arms. She seems indifferent when he says he has *the book*. In bed together, they hear the red-armed washerwoman singing. Julia is sleepy but Winston insists on opening the book and reading it to her aloud. He goes back to the first chapter.

In dramatic terms, Orwell has stopped his story cold again to teach us more about totalitarian theory. Because he's still very much a novelist, he makes this lull in dramatic action function as a lull in the story. He is also introducing detail that will work dramatically in *Part Three*.

NOTE:

1. The long reading postpones Winston's downfall, giving us a chance to worry about him and be angry with him for lying here reading when he ought to be planning an escape. He and Julia are already established as doomed lovers; they have taken the final risk by meeting O'Brien and accepting the book. Unless they're going to try to escape, there isn't much left for Orwell to tell. It won't serve his purpose to let them get away, and it may be that, as a novelist, he was feeling too rushed by his failing health to have the time or energy to describe even an unsuccessful escape attempt. He certainly intended to have Winston's story end as it does—but not yet.

2. He needs this detailed description of Party thinking to set up *Part Three*, in which Winston and O'Brien are locked in mental battle. Keep in mind Goldstein's points as O'Brien and Winston tangle in *Part Three*, and look for the irony involved as O'Brien reveals who really wrote the book.

You may want to decide how you regard this extract: as a story-wrecker or as an essential part of the book. Either position is respectable. Think about it as Winston goes on reading.

Chapter 1

IGNORANCE IS STRENGTH

Orwell repeats the paragraph dividing society into High, Middle and Low orders, adding: "The aims of these three groups are entirely irreconcilable. The aim of the High is to remain where they are. The aim of the Middle is to change places with the High. The aim of the Low, when they have an aim . . . is to abolish all distinctions and create a society in which all men shall be equal."

Goldstein believes the Low order is too crushed by drudgery to have time for such thought. He sees history as a cyclical process—continuing struggle in which the High is overthrown by the Middle, aided by the Low. The Middle takes over, becomes the High, and then suppresses the Low. A new Middle group splits off from the Low or Middle group to challenge the High and the cycle begins again.

As you follow Goldstein's argument, try to decide whether this essentially pessimistic view is a true picture of the world as it is today. It's possible to argue both ways—to say that yes, this is the way of the world, or no, we are progressing toward a better society. An essential question asked by Goldstein's book is whether humanity is better off now than, say, a hundred years ago, or than it will be in the future.

Goldstein writes that the average human is physically better off, but "no advance in wealth, no softening of manners, no reform or revolution has ever brought human equality a millimeter nearer." For the Low, there is only the occasional change in masters.

By the late 19th century, Goldstein says, many thinkers pointed to this cyclical process as evidence that inequality was built into the nature of life. In the past the High had claimed the need for a hierarchical society to support its position of power. The Middle, which had used concepts of freedom, justice and fraternity to justify its bid for power, were going to have to adjust their rhetoric to allow for the cyclical theory. How could they promise equality to a Low order if history proclaimed that there would always be a Low order? They had to adjust their thinking, too. If technology made true equality possible, they would lose all their power.

Although Socialism was established to create liberty and equality (the Utopian, or perfect society), the new Middle groups would make changes in it. Their aim? To keep power once they got it. The new movements, Goldstein writes, aimed to perpetuate *un*freedom and *in*equality, to freeze history. Once the cycle was complete and the Middle became High, they intended to stay High. The new, powerful parties Goldstein names are Ingsoc (English Socialism) in Oceania, Neo-Bolshevism in Eurasia, and Death-worship in East-asia.

NOTE: On Socialism

In a letter written at the time, Orwell made it plain that he was not attacking English Socialism or the British Labor party. He was angered by Fascism (strong national government under a dictator) in Germany and Spain, and by the perversion of socialist ideals in Stalinist Russia. He wanted through exaggeration to point out the dangers of totalitarian ideas because, he said, "I believe that totalitarian ideas have taken root in the minds of intellectuals everywhere."

Socialism is a political and economic theory of organization based on collective or governmental ownership of the means of producing and distributing goods and services. Today the government in England operates health care services, transportation, mining and some radio and TV programming, among other things. Orwell feared government control pushed too far would endanger human freedom.

Warning people about totalitarianism in other countries, Orwell wanted people in democratic countries to be aware of the grim possibilities raised when they delegated too much authority to their own governments.

For groups who had recently seized power, Goldstein continues, the possibility raised by the machine age of real equality presented a danger. In order to solidify their control, the new governments, beginning around 1930, became harshly authoritarian. They resorted to imprisonment without trial, the use of war prisoners as slaves, public executions, torture, the deportation (Hitler's treatment of the Jews, for example) of entire populations.

The new High order, according to Goldstein, is made up of bureaucrats, scientists, publicity experts and other middle- and upper-middle working-class people hungry for pure power and ruthless in their attempts to gain it. Compared to the old ruling class, they're unaffected by liberal ideas, and brutally efficient. Aided by print, TV and film, they have used propaganda and surveillance to expand their influence and to suppress private thoughts and actions.

This group consolidated its position through collectivism, or the abolition of private property, according to Goldstein. By abolishing private property, the new High order concentrated it in far fewer hands than before—their own. Collectively, he says, the Party in Oceania owns everything because it controls everything, and disposes of the products as it thinks fit.

The Party accomplished this by "collectivizing," taking over factories, mines, land, houses, transport in the name of Socialism. INGSOC "has in fact carried out the main item in the Socialist program, with the result . . . that economic inequality has been made permanent."

A ruling group, says Goldstein, can fall from power:

1.   By being conquered from outside.

2.   By a revolt of the masses.

3.   By permitting a strong, discontented Middle group to develop.

4.   By losing self-confidence and the will to rule.

A ruling class with a strong enough desire to rule can remain in power permanently, Goldstein says. The existence of superstates (WAR IS PEACE) eliminates the possibility of being conquered from outside. Since the masses have no basis for comparison, they don't know they're oppressed and won't revolt. Continuous warfare maintains morale and keeps out people from other societies.

The only remaining dangers to the Party are the rise of the Middle group and "the growth of liberalism and skepticism in their own ranks." To eliminate these dangers, society is organized as a pyramid. At its top is Big Brother, the infallible and adored figure created to focus the love, fear and reverence of the people. Next comes the Inner Party, the "brain" of the State. Next is the Outer Party, or "hands." At the base of the pyramid are the proles.

In principle anybody can enter any branch of the Party. The rulers are held together by belief in INGSOC and its aims. In fact, however, there's less mobility than there was in the old days of capitalism. Since membership is not passed down according to blood lines, the Party pretends to be above "class privilege"; but few people move from one group to another. Why not? The Party sees to it.

The Party perpetuates itself and its power by naming its successors. In order to remain in power forever, the Party keeps the proles in a state of ignorance and uses Thought Police to monitor Party members and prevent independent thought—and therefore questions about the system.

Thought Police make sure Party members hold the right opinions and have the right instincts by watching them constantly and weeding out anybody who deviates from the Party norm. From childhood Party members are trained in:

1. *Crimestop*, or "protective stupidity"; in other words, stopping short of any dangerous thought.

2. *Blackwhite*, or thinking of Big Brother as omnipotent and the Party as infallible even when they're not. This implies discipline—saying black is white if ordered. It also means *believing* it.

3. *Doublethink*, or holding two contradictory beliefs at the same time, and believing both of them. This makes possible the alteration of the past (what Winston does at the office). With no past to compare things with, everybody is satisfied with present-day conditions. More important, changing the records safeguards the infallibility of the Party, removing from the records any hint that the Party was ever wrong about anything.

This ability to change the past is central to INGSOC. In controlling the past, the Party controls the minds of its members. Since the Party possesses absolute truth, memories have to be trained to forget the old and accept the new through *doublethink*. The trick is to combine belief in Party infallibility with the power to learn from past mistakes. This makes for many contradictions, which are at the heart of Party rule. The

Party is built on unreality, or "controlled insanity." Insane people don't ask dangerous questions.

Why, Goldstein asks, should human equality be prevented, and at such cost? This is the central secret, which consists. . . .

We're not going to get the answer to this one. Winston—who, as you may have forgotten by now, is reading all this aloud to Julia—gives her a poke. Is she awake?

The clever girl has dozed off. Winston snuggles down, thinking he knows *how* life became so terrible, but not *why*. We've been led to believe the answer is in the very next sentence, but Orwell has chosen to keep the answer from us and from Winston. He feels sleepy, confident, safe, and falls asleep murmuring, "Sanity is not statistical." His crime, then, is being sane enough to keep asking questions—and he will pay.

SECTION X

Winston wakes to a cold stove and to the prole woman singing in the courtyard. Julia joins him at the window and together they stare down at her. "It had never before occurred to him that the body of a woman of fifty . . . coarse in the grain like an overripe turnip, could be beautiful." Now it does. He slips his arm around Julia's slim waist, and laments that they will never have a child. The woman down there may have no mind, he thinks, but she has "strong arms, a warm heart, and a fertile belly." He imagines the woman bearing children, grandchildren, in a sort of "mystical reverence" that extends to the sky and all the people under it. He concludes that the future belongs to the proles, and thinks this must be Goldstein's secret. Winston believes that the proles are immortal and that in the end they will awake and build a new society. But even in this mystical reverie, he seems somewhat condescending to the lower orders. "Out of those mighty loins a race of conscious beings must one day come," he says. "You were the dead; theirs was the future."

"We are the dead," say both Winston and Julia. And then a third voice knifes into the room, saying, "You are the dead." This is the voice of doom Winston foresaw when he started the diary.

The telescreen was behind the picture of St. Clement's Dane that Winston was so fond of, and that Julia had wanted to take down and give a good cleaning. The print crashes from the wall and Winston thinks: "It was starting, it was starting at last!" He seems excited. Outside is the tramping of boots. A thin, cultivated voice Winston thinks he recognizes completes the old nursery rhyme: *Here comes a candle to light you to bed, here comes a chopper to chop off your head!*

A ladder crashes through the window and troops enter, uniformed in black, wearing iron-shod boots and carrying clubs. They look very much like Hitler's storm troopers. As they threaten Winston, one of them smashes the paperweight, and the bit of coral at the center tumbles out. How small, Winston thinks, how small it always was! The world of the paperweight, which was the world of the past where everything was beautiful and where Winston imagined he was safe, is shattered.

Winston is kicked; Julia is beaten and carried away, her face already yellow and contorted. Winston is confused by the old-fashioned clock; because it's numbered one to twelve, he doesn't know whether it's "twenty-thirty" that afternoon or "nought eight-thirty" the next morning. The past has ceased to be of use to him.

Mr. Charrington now appears; it was his voice that completed the nursery rhyme. He's no longer dear old Mr. Charrington; he has shed his disguise and revealed himself as a member of the Thought Police.

NOTE: The purpose and effectiveness of the long extract from Goldstein's book at this crucial point in the novel is going to be debated as long as *1984* is read. Now is a good time to pinpoint your own responses to it. Many of you will defend it hotly; others will argue, with justification, that it breaks the back of the novel. Ask yourselves, did you:

1. Have an easy or a hard time following it?

2. Think it was the right length, or too long?

3. Need the political background to understand conditions in the novel?

4. Consider it an isolated sermon, or an essential part of the novel?

PART THREE

SECTION I

Winston is in a cell. As you read about his imprisonment you may want to compare it to current news reports about the plight of political prisoners in certain countries in Latin America and Eastern Europe.

Winston's cell is bright and bare and monitored by four telescreens. Voices bark instructions whenever he moves—even when he puts his hand in his pocket for food. He has lost track of time. He hasn't eaten. He has been moved from a filthy, crowded holding cell where a huge wreck of a woman was hurled into his lap, hoisted herself off and began vomiting. Her last name is Smith too, and in one of the strangest moments in the book she says, "I might be your mother," and Winston believes this may be the truth.

It's hard to know whether this is just a surreal touch or an attempt on Orwell's part to acknowledge how close he (and Winston) may really be to the Low order. Does he want us to believe that Party torture has reduced Winston's mother to this terrible state? He does, at least, want us to believe such things are possible in this nightmare world.

Winston can't concentrate. Beaten by his captors, he can't keep his mind on Julia. He thinks of O'Brien with a flickering hope. The Brotherhood is supposed to send a razor blade to members who are captured— this would let them escape through death. He understands that in this place the lights are never turned out. So here at last is the "place where there is no darkness!"

An officer hurls Ampleforth, a poet, into Winston's cell. He's imprisoned for leaving the word "God" in a *Newspeak* translation of Kipling. Soon after, Ampleforth is marched off to the dreaded room 101.

A procession of prisoners now passes through this cell, including Winston's tubby neighbor Parsons, who is grimly proud that his daughter turned him in for Thoughtcrime before he did anything worse. Parsons sits himself down on the toilet and leaves behind a disgusting smell. This is one of a procession of gross physical details Orwell uses to make us understand

and sympathize with Winston's position. We see a starving man; a chinless man spitting blood, saliva and false teeth after being hit; guards breaking a man's fingers as they drag him off to Room 101.

Winston fears for Julia and believes but does not "feel" that he would double his own pain to save her. "In this place," he realizes, "you could not feel anything, except pain and the foreknowledge of pain."

The door opens and O'Brien enters. Winston assumes O'Brien has been caught, but O'Brien says ironically, "They got me a long time ago." He isn't a prisoner, he's one of the captors. "You knew this," he tells Winston. "Don't deceive yourself . . . you have always known it."

Winston knows this is true.

When a guard smashes Winston's elbow, he realizes he could never wish more pain, even to save Julia, because in the face of pain there are no heroes. He falls to the floor.

NOTE: In these pages and the pages to come we'll see the strange fascination Winston has for O'Brien, and we'll see how he behaves under torture. Look back at the questions raised about both Winston and O'Brien in the CHARACTERS section of this guide. Does Winston have a death wish that is at work here, or does he behave like a man who would rather die than live under this kind of oppression? Either point of view can be defended, even though the fact that Winston has always known O'Brien was in the party indicates that he did bring his capture down upon himself. What do you think his motives were?

SECTION II

Winston wakes up after a series of beatings and torture sessions in which he confessed to crimes he never committed. His memories are confused with hallucinations in which he confesses everything and is forgiven. O'Brien was with him the whole time, directing everything, orchestrating the pain.

A voice—he thinks it's O'Brien's—has said, "Don't worry, Winston; you are in my keeping. For seven years I have watched over you. Now the turning point has come. I shall save you, I shall make you perfect." It is the same voice that told him they would meet in the place where there is no darkness. Another of Winston's dreams is coming true.

Now O'Brien is looking down at him. He told Winston they would meet here, he says, and with a twist of a dial, floods Winston's body with pain. He intends to help Winston remember events as the Party says they took place. This means he has to forget about the about-face during Hate Week, when the Party suddenly changed enemies from Eurasia to Eastasia; and he has to forget everything about Jones, Aaronson and Rutherford. O'Brien himself already believes that Oceania has always been at war with Eastasia, and that Jones and the others were always enemies of the state.

This is doublethink.

O'Brien has Winston repeat the Party slogan: "Who controls the past controls the future; who controls the present controls the past." The past, he explains, exists only in written records controlled by the Party and in memories *controlled by the Party*. This is the heart of doublethink.

Winston is being punished because, lacking humility and self-discipline, he did not allow his memories to be controlled. "You would not make the act of submission, which is the price of sanity," he is told. "Reality exists in the human mind, and nowhere else." The mind, of course, is not the individual mind, but the mind of the Party, "which is collective and immortal." The only truth is the Party's truth. O'Brien reminds Winston of his fatal diary entry—that freedom means being able to say two and two makes four. Using torture, he tries to get Winston to say that two and two make five—because the Party says so.

Winston's resistance finally breaks down, and when he agrees that two plus two make anything O'Brien wants them to make, O'Brien stops the pain and helps him sit up. Winston now clings to O'Brien like a baby, allowing himself to be comforted by O'Brien's strong arm. He has the idea that the pain is coming from somewhere else and that O'Brien is going to save him.

Winston weeps. You'll have to try harder, O'Brien says, because it's not easy to become sane. And so the torture begins again, the pain now even more intense as O'Brien holds up his fingers, asking how many Winston sees. When Winston finally admits he no longer knows, O'Brien is pleased, and the pain stops. Winston now feels great love for O'Brien, partly becaused he stopped the pain, and partly because O'Brien, whether friend or enemy, is "a person who could be talked to." Being loved may not be the important thing, Winston thinks; what may be more important is being understood. The last (thinking) man in Europe may at last have what he has always wanted—somebody he can really talk to.

Winston behaves like the neglected child who does

something naughty to get attention. Some kids would rather be punished than ignored; Winston may be one of them.

O'Brien verifies that Winston suspected, that they are deep inside the Ministry of Love. The authorities have brought him here not only to make him confess and to punish him, but to make him sane. What Goldstein's book called "controlled insanity," the Party calls sanity. It does more than destroy its enemies, it changes them.

For the first time, O'Brien seems ugly to Winston. O'Brien also looks mad.

In a long speech O'Brien explains that the Party has no room for martyrs. The Inquisition in the Middle Ages was a failure because it killed its enemies publicly. Resistance brought glory to the victims. O'Brien points out that the Nazis and the Russian Communists were more cruel and efficient than the Inquisitors because they knew martyrs only perpetuated a cause.

The Nazis and the Soviets did their best to discredit their victims before they came to trial. Yet these victims still became martyrs in time when the public realized that confessions were made under torture. As for confessions made to the Party? "We make them true," says O'Brien. The future will not make a martyr of Winston because the future will never hear of him. He will become an *unperson*.

Why then does the Party bother to interrogate him? Because, O'Brien explains, he's a flaw in the pattern—something that has to be erased. First they will convert him to their beliefs, make him one of them. They will wash him clean of rebellion and they will dispose of him only after his mind is clean. He will be dead inside, so completely destroyed that he could not recover in a thousand years. "We shall squeeze you empty and fill you with ourselves."

At a signal from O'Brien, Winston is attached to a new instrument O'Brien says isn't going to hurt. A devastating explosion fills his head instead: a blinding light that flattens him and seems to take a large piece out of his brain.

NOTE: In the 1940s, when Orwell was writing, mental patients were given "shock treatments" in which they were zapped with electricity to alter mental states; Orwell may have had this in mind.

When O'Brien asks Winston what country Oceania is at war with, what happened to Jones, etc., and how many fingers he is holding up, Winston says what O'Brien wants him to say and sees what O'Brien wants him to see. He even sees five fingers instead of four.

O'Brien is pleased that Winston is coming along, and praises him. Winston's mind appeals to him; he enjoys talking to him because they are alike except, of course, that Winston is insane. Does Winston have any questions?

Yes. He wants to know about Julia.

She betrayed you at once—wholeheartedly, O'Brien says. All her rebelliousness, her folly, and "her dirty-mindedness" have been burned out of her.

Winston next wants to know if Big Brother exists, even as he, Winston, exists. O'Brien points out coldly that Winston does not exist. What about the Brotherhood? O'Brien tells him that's a riddle that will forever remain unsolved. What's in Room 101? O'Brien tells him that he already knows—everybody knows what's in Room 101—and then he puts Winston to sleep.

SECTION III

Winston has been interrogated for days, perhaps weeks. He has learned how to avoid the pain by giving the right answers. O'Brien reminds him that he wrote in his diary that he understood *how* the society worked, but not *why*. If phase one of his brainwashing was learning, the next two are understanding and acceptance. O'Brien is about to tell him *why*.

Nobody seems very surprised that O'Brien collaborated on Goldstein's book. Its program, to educate the proles to overthrow the party, is nonsense. The rule of the Party is forever, O'Brien says. Why? Winston says what he believes to be the Party line—that the Party rules over people for their own good. It's the wrong answer.

O'Brien punishes him at once. The Party, he says, seeks power for its own sake. Power is an end in itself. He notices that Winston is looking at his aging face and admits that yes, he will get old and die, but he is only one cell in an organism that will never die. Power is collective. Together, Party members can rule. They control matter because they control the mind: "Reality is inside the skull. . . . We make the laws of nature."

Winston takes the side of nature and argues that the age of the earth and the existence of the stars prove that physical reality is beyond man's control. O'Brien is indifferent. Stars are only bits of fire, he says; the Party could reach them if it wanted to; it could blot them out. When it's convenient, the Party believes the earth revolves around the sun. But at other times the earth becomes the center of the universe. Doublethink makes it possible.

O'Brien points out that the Party's real power is not over things, but over men, and that its power is both exercised and demonstrated by making them suffer. O'Brien's theory of power is not based on happiness, as in most Utopian visions of the perfect society. It is based on sadism. The Party will dissolve the family and do away with sex, art, literature, and science. "If you want a picture of the future," writes Orwell, "imagine a boot stamping on a human face—forever."

Some readers question whether the Party's motivation is strong or believable enough. Many totalitarian governments use force to carry out their aims, but only as a means to other ends? O'Brien claims Party members aren't interested in pleasure, luxury, or privilege; all they want is to govern totally and inflict pain. Is this convincing? You can argue either way.

Winston thinks it is not convincing. He says it's impossible for civilizations founded on fear, hatred and cruelty to survive. He has to believe that something—the human spirit, perhaps—will defeat them.

O'Brien tells Winston that his kind is extinct. He may be the "last" man, but he is completely alone, and he is by no means superior. He makes Winston strip and then leads him to a mirror. For the first time since his capture, Winston sees himself naked and cries out.

Some people have suggested that the description of Winston here—a bag of bones, gray all over with dirt, with falling hair and teeth coming out—was influenced by Orwell's own physical deterioration; he was dying of TB. Winston looks at himself and weeps. He blames O'Brien for bringing him to this awful state.

No, O'Brien points out. Nothing has happened that Winston didn't foresee. When he defied the Party by beginning the diary, he brought destruction upon himself.

Winston has been broken and humiliated, but he has not betrayed Julia. O'Brien acknowledges this and Winston is overwhelmed with reverence for him—with gratitude for his intelligence. In spite of all his confessions, he hasn't stopped loving Julia. O'Brien admits that it may be a long time before they shoot Winston, since he's such a difficult case. But everyone is "cured" sooner or later, he says reassuringly; and in the end they will shoot him.

SECTION IV

Weeks or months have passed. Winston is getting fatter, his room has been made more comfortable. He dozes, dreaming happily of the Golden Country, of his mother, of Julia and O'Brien. He is relatively content. Being fed, clean, and unmolested are enough. As he gets better, he does a few pushups and begins to write on a slate.

At this point, he realized the foolishness of his single-handed attempt to oppose the party, and thinks he has given up. He knows the Thought Police have watched him for seven years, and that they have photographs and know everything about him. All he has to do is learn how to think as they think. He writes:

FREEDOM IS SLAVERY.

He writes:

TWO AND TWO MAKE FIVE.

But he can't keep from writing:

GOD IS POWER.

He believes he has accepted everything, that the laws of nature are nonsense, that everything the Party says is true. He tries to train himself to believe everything the Party says, no matter how ridiculous. Yet he still has to exercise *crimestop* and stop himself from asking treasonable questions.

In the meantime he wonders how soon they will shoot him. He daydreams about the moment, about walking down the corridor, waiting for the bullet in his back. The inevitability of death releases him from doubt, and makes him certain and strong. He imagines himself walking into the Golden Country of his dreams and memories. Before his capture, the Golden Country existed in the past for Winston; now it belongs to the release of death; it is a vision perhaps of heaven. Suddenly he shouts Julia's name. He loves her more than ever.

He has undone himself. The guards, knowing that, in spite of all his obedience, he still hates the Party, will be at the door in seconds. He has surrendered with his mind, but not his heart. The brainwashing will begin all over again, but he is determined, no matter what they do, to keep his inner self alive. They will shoot him one day but he will still hate them all.

To die hating them, he thinks, will be freedom.

O'Brien and the guards arrive. What does Winston think of Big Brother? Winston confesses that he hates him. O'Brien says it's time for Winston to take the last step. It is not enough to obey Big Brother, Winston must love him. O'Brien orders Winston to Room 101. Winston's last dream is about to come true: for this is the dark place with something terrible waiting for him, just out of sight.

SECTION V

Here is where Winston has been heading all along: to the room that contains that which he fears most. Remember how horrified he was at Mr. Charrington's, when Julia chased a rat?

Ever since *1984* was published people have argued whether the horrors of Room 101 are really horrible or only anticlimactic. Orwell used what he thought was the grossest and most disgusting image imaginable, because he was trying to communicate Winston's state of mind, and the ultimate horror of totalitarian methods.

The experience in Room 101 is supposed to destroy Winston's last shred of resistance. In trying to understand his reaction, it's useful for you to think how you would respond to a similar kind of torture.

Winston is strapped in a chair with his head clamped so it can't move. O'Brien comes in. On the table is a cage with a handle and a mask at one end. O'Brien knows that Winston's worst fear is rats. He reminds Winston of his nightmare, in which everything was black and there was something terrible on the other side of the wall. Since pain alone has not done the job on Winston, O'Brien will rely on Winston's instinct for survival. Faced with the rats, Winston will do what O'Brien wants. He doesn't have to be told what that is.

O'Brien is going to put the cage with the rats on Winston's head and let them eat his face. He clicks the first lever. Winston fights panic and at the last minute loses his reason in the desperate urge to save himself. He shouts, over and over: "Do it to Julia! Not me!"

This is the final betrayal of self that O'Brien wants, and Winston is released.

SECTION VI

Winston is at the Chestnut Tree, the haven for released political prisoners. He's in his usual corner, getting drunk on Victory Gin and watching the news on the telescreen. He can still smell the rats, although he doesn't name them even in his thoughts.

This is a fatter, coarser-looking Winston, listless and so fuzzy-headed that everything the Party says is fine with him. Note how different Winston's condition is from that of Orwell, who put off going to the hospital when he was dying so that he could finish his message of warning to the world.

Winston traces on the table: 2+2=5. The Party has finally won him—forever. The most private and important part of himself has been destroyed.

The Party has destroyed Julia, too. The last time Winston saw her, on a miserable, cold day, she too had changed. He had put his arm around her waist, knowing the Party had stopped watching them. The idea of sex revolted him because her waist had become thick and stiff as a corpse's. She looked at him with dislike, perhaps because of their past, perhaps because he too had changed physically.

They sat down and exchanged confessions. Both had betrayed each other at the last minute in order to save themselves from torture. They even *wanted* each other to be tortured! "All you care about is yourself," Julia said, and Winston agreed.

After they parted, half-heartedly agreeing to meet again, Winston followed her for a moment, but then returned anxiously to the warmth and safety of the Chestnut Tree Cafe. He lost track of her quickly: "Perhaps her thickened, stiffened body was no longer recognizable from behind." Yes, he had betrayed her; he had wished she would be given to the—The telescreen cuts off this thought, as a voice sings the refrain we remember:

> *Under the spreading chestnut tree*
> *I sold you and you sold me—*

It's the song they were playing the day he saw the three political prisoners here in the Chestnut Tree Cafe. He weeps and has another gin, which is what he now needs to get through the day. He is teased by a sudden memory of his mother just before she disappeared; he and his sister are fussing, and his mother goes out to buy him a toy. They laugh and are happy, playing Snakes and Ladders. This must be a false memory, Winston tells himself, and he pushes it out of his mind.

The telescreen trumpets a victory in the unending war and Winston looks at the picture of Big Brother. The portrait makes him feel glad. He has undergone great changes since he first went to the Ministry of Love, but the final moment of healing takes place at this moment.

As the war news continues Winston daydreams that he is back in the Ministry, forgiven, his soul white as snow. He is traveling down the long white corridor of his daydreams when the longawaited bullet enters his brain.

Back in the cafe, he looks up at Big Brother's face. It has taken him forty years to get here, to learn how to win this victory over himself, but it is accomplished.

Winston has learned to love Big Brother.

APPENDIX

This is a mock-scholarly article about the official language of Oceania, which was expected to supersede standard English around 2050. It is designed to express the proper thoughts necessary for Party members, and also to make all other modes of thought impossible by depriving the language of certain words. The new language has three vocabularies.

1. The A vocabulary includes words for everyday activities such as eating, drinking, working. It contains simple nouns and verbs with unequivocal meanings, like *tree* and *hit*. Any shades of meaning have been purged. The grammar is designed so that any word can be used as a verb, noun, adjective or adverb. By adding prefixes and suffixes, users can change a word's meaning. *Uncold* is *warm; doubleplus cold* means extremely cold. Anything difficult to pronounce has been eliminated.

2. The B vocabulary includes words deliberately constructed for political purposes. They're designed to promote "right" thoughts. Words such as *justice, democracy* and *religion* have been abolished, or reduced to either *crimethink* or *oldthink.* Names of government organizations and arms of the state like *thinkpol* (Thought Police) fall into this grouping. Words such as *Communist International,* Orwell felt, called up thoughts of human brotherhood, and images of thinker Karl Marx, whereas the then current word *Comintern* suggested a tightly knit organization with a precise doctrine. The intention of Newspeak, he says, is to make speech, especially on any subject not ideologically neutral, as nearly automatic and thoughtless as possible.

3. The C vocabulary includes scientific and technical terms, purged of any ideological meaning. The aim was to keep knowledge specialized and compartmentalized so nobody would know too much.

Once Oldspeak is altogether superseded, the last link with the history and literature of the past will be broken. The Declaration of Independence, for instance, would be untranslatable. The closest translation would be one word: *crimethink*.

A STEP BEYOND

Tests and Answers

TESTS

Test 1

1. Newspeak   _____
   A. is a commentary on current events
   B. is more ambiguous than Standard English
   C. made it almost impossible to express unorthodox opinions

2. Now that we have reached the year 1984, Orwell's novel   _____
   A. seems to have proven false as a prophecy
   B. has served its purpose in helping to avert the nightmare world he described
   C. remains useful in warning of the consequences of totalitarianism

3. *1984*   _____
   A. is an anti-Utopian novel
   B. shows the political realities facing world leaders
   C. presents a fable of the unquenchable spark of freedom even in an oppressed society

4. "The Theory and Practice of Oligarchal Collectivism" was written by   _____
   A. Emmanuel Goldstein
   B. Big Brother
   C. Comrade Ogilvy

5. The least influential group in the society of
   1984 is
   A. The Inner Party
   B. The Proles
   C. The Outer Party

6. Winston Smith's first act of rebellion is his   _____
   A. denouncing O'Brien
   B. taking Julia as a mistress
   C. writing in a diary

7. One of the Party slogans is: Ignorance is   _____
   A. Knowledge
   B. Strength
   C. Defeat

8. Oceania is in a state of war   _____
   A. to acquire economic benefits through
      victory
   B. to foster patriotism and devotion to the
      Party
   C. to maintain the status quo

9. Winston Smith's job at the Ministry of Truth   _____
   involves
   A. altering past history to make it conform
      to Party doctrine
   B. investigating those suspected of
      betraying the Party
   C. writing propaganda to promote Party
      loyalty

10. The Brotherhood   _____
    A. acts as the secret arm of the Party
       engaged in "internal police work"
    B. seeks to overthrow Big Brother
    C. provides opportunity for social contacts
       for the Party elite

11. Write about *1984* as Orwell's political message to the world. Why was it so important to him?

12. Is *1984* successful as fiction?

13. Write about George Orwell's view of sex, and of women in particular, as demonstrated in *1984*.

14. How does Orwell use objects as symbols in telling his story?

15. How does the political concept of revisionism enter into the world of *1984*?

Test 2

1. Winston Smith meets Ampleforth and   _____
   Parsons in the
   A. Ministry of Love
   B. Ministry of Truth
   C. Ministry of Peace

2. Mr. Charrington is   _____
   A. a poet apprehended by the Thought
      Police because he rhymed the word "rod"
      with the suspect word "God"
   B. a disguised agent of the Thought Police
   C. one of the three men executed as traitors

3. The prescribed antidote for Thoughtcrime   _____
   was
   A. Confession
   B. Doublethink
   C. Crimestop

4. The laws in the society of *1984* are   _____
   A. clearly enumerated in "The Theory and
      Practice of Oligarchal Collectivism"
   B. constantly being explained by Big Brother
   C. not written down

5. O'Brien _____
   A. proves to be Winston's undoing
   B. is the only ray of light in Winston's
      dreary life
   C. encourages the illicit affair between Julia
      and Winston

6. The shortage of material comforts and goods _____
   in Oceania is
   A. blamed by the Party on the war
   B. contradicted by the statistics on the telescreen
   C. denied by Winston in his discussion
      with Parsons

7. Winston's sexual encounter with Julia is _____
   considered a serious offense because
   A. it followed Winston's experience with
      the Prole prostitute
   B. Winston's marriage to Katherine had not
      yet produced a child for the Party
   C. both are Party members

8. The glass paperweight that is smashed by _____
   the policeman
   A. symbolizes the beautiful, self-
      contained world of the past
   B. is given to Julia as an expression of
      Winston's love
   C. is used as evidence to incriminate Winston

9. Winston's downfall _____
   A. is a direct result of his attempt to seek
      privacy
   B. is the culmination of a complex
      surveillance that he has been subjected to
      since the "disappearance" of his parents
   C. can be traced to his belief that he can
      "beat the system"

10. The final scene of *1984* takes place in   ____
    A. Room 101
    B. the cellar of the Ministry of Truth
    C. the Chestnut Tree Cafe

11. What is Orwell's view of the common people, as demonstrated by his treatment of the *proles?*

12. What is the importance of the character O'Brien in *1984?*

13. Using what you have learned of Winston's life, write about the differences between the world of *1984* and life in America today.

14. Write about Winston Smith as a person, using what you know about him from reading about him in *1984*, giving three examples.

15. WAR IS PEACE, FREEDOM IS SLAVERY, IGNORANCE IS STRENGTH. What do these slogans mean in *1984?*

ANSWERS

Test 1

1. C   2. C   3. A   4. A   5. C   6. C

7. B   8. C   9. A   10. B

Parts of the book you'll want to refer to in answering the essay questions are labeled *One, Two, Three,* with sections numbered *I, II,* etc. For example, *One, IV* means *Part One, Section IV.*

11. You'll want to remind your reader that Orwell was worried about the march of Communism in Stalinist Russia, and about the rise of Fascism in Hitler's Germany and Franco's Spain (see The Author and His Times). He also worried about English Socialism and feared that, if a government got too much power in any country, hu-

man freedom would disappear. You can use examples of Party surveillance (the telescreens, Thought Police, Ministry of Love) and enforcement from *One, I–IV* to demonstrate how Orwell delivered his message. You can describe events from Winston's life in *One* and *Two* to show how loss of individual freedom affects one man.

12. You can write about how Winston's story affected you. Did you care about him and Julia? Were you sympathetic to them and worried about their fate when they began their love affair?

    Look at The Characters section for ways to develop your answer. The section on Form and Structure will help you decide whether the inclusion of the long extract of political writing *(Two, IX)* and the *Appendix* helped or hurt the novel.

    Specific examples of the way Winston thinks about Julia and the way he treats her are in *Parts One* and *Two* of the novel, particularly in *One, I* and *II;* and *Two, I, IV* and *V.* You'll want to use these examples if you have to write about how the love story affected you. They will also be useful for your discussion of the next question too.

13. There are fairly extensive descriptions of the Party's use of sexual sublimation to promote war fever in *One, I;* of Winston's thoughts on motherhood and the dark-haired girl in *One, III,* and on prostitutes and marriage in *One, IV.* Using these sections, you can make a fairly strong case that Winston is a sexist who divides women into two classes—mothers, who are not sexual, and sexual women, who are "bad," and therefore attractive. You may want to draw conclusions from this about the author as well. As you develop your answer, look at the sections listed in the last paragraph of Question 2 to see how Winston thinks about Julia, and how he treats her.

14. You can refer to the telescreen described in *One, I* and used everywhere throughout the novel (look especially at *Two, VIII*) as a symbol or a demonstration of Party oppression. Equally important are *(a)* the engraving of St. Clement's Dane which Winston sees in *One, VIII* at Mr. Charrington's and which figures importantly during his capture in *Two, IX;* and *(b)* the paperweight, both a symbol of the past when Winston buys it in *One, VIII* and a symbol of the destruction of Winston's world in *Two, IX,* when the paperweight is shattered at the time of his capture.

15. Look at the extensive description of Winston's job in *One, II* (see Note at end of the section,) and especially *One, III* to see how the Party rewrites history for its purposes. The rapid about-face as the enemy changes in the middle of Hate Week (*Two*, opening of *IX*) shows this happening. In *Two, IX* in "Goldstein's" book which Winston is reading, you will see not only how history is rewritten, but why.

As you'll see in *Two IX*, the Party rewrites history in order to maintain power. Rewriting the past allows the Party to keep members ignorant of any mistakes the Party might have made and removes any basis for comparison with either the past or other societies.

Test 2

1. A   2. B   3. C   4. C   5. A   6. B

7. C   8. A   9. B   10. C

Parts of the book you'll want to refer to in answering the essay questions are labeled *One, Two, Three*, with sections numbered *I, II*, etc. For example, *One, IV* means *Part One, Section IV*.

11. It seems clear that Orwell both envied the common people for their uncomplicated lives (we see this as Winston goes among them in *One, VIII*) and doubted their capacity to better themselves. In *One, VI* and *VIII* and *Two, VII* we see that Winston rather envies the *proles* because of their mindless, somewhat animal-like existence. By *Two, IX*, he's looking to them as the hope for the future. You can write about his encounter with the *prole* mob, remembered in *One, VIII*, and his talk with the old man in that same section. Looking carefully at his thoughts about the *prole* woman (after the Goldstein sections of *Two, IX*), will help you pull together your thoughts about how both the author and Winston are depressed and attracted by the lower classes.

12. A. You can write about Winston's fascination for O'Brien as shown in *One, I*, when Winston first thinks about him and remembers the dream, and in the last few lines of *One, VII*. Look at their meeting in *Two, III* to see what kind of hypnotic effect O'Brien has on Winston. The reasons for this fascination are demonstrated in *Part Three*.

B. You can write about O'Brien as a symbol of the totalitarian way of thinking by picking any of his and Winston's scenes in *Three*, especially *Three, II*.

C. Consider O'Brien as representing the upper classes to both Orwell and Winston as you look at *Two, VIII*. His luxurious apartment, his lordly manner and his effect on Winston all help demonstrate his position. Winston's attraction to O'Brien after he is captured (*Three, II*) indicates that he's happy to have an upper class person to talk to in spite of the torture.

13. You can find details in *One, I* and *One, VIII* that describe Winston's daily life and his surroundings. Look at his love affair in *One, I*, when he first sees the dark-haired girl; in *One, III*, when he dreams about her; and in *Two,*

II and *V*, when their relationship develops. This will give you the necessary background to compare Winston's affair to the lives of lovers today. A comparative study of governments—theirs and ours—can be made after reading *One*, *III* and *IV* and *Three*, *I* and *II*. Look at *One*, *I*, *III* and most other sections for descriptions of the use of television (the telescreen), which you can compare to the use of TV today.

14. A. Write about Winston as a rebel, basing your opinions on material in *One*, *I* when he begins his affair with Julia; in *Two*, *II*, when he thinks of his affair as rebellion against the state; in *Two*, *VIII*, when he meets O'Brien and vows to overthrow Big Brother; and in *Three*, *II*, *III* and *IV*, when he tries to resist brainwashing.

B. Write about Winston as lover, using *Two*, *IV* to show his tenderness toward Julia, and *Three*, *V*—when they meet again after they've been brainwashed—to show how sadly the affair has ended.

C. Write about Winston as 20th-century intellectual man in conflict with the society by looking at his dialogues with O'Brien after he's captured in *Three*, *II*, *III*, *IV*.

15. WAR IS PEACE is explained in *Two*, *IX*, at the end of the first long section of the book by Emmanuel Goldstein that Winston is reading. So long as there is a limited war which nobody wins, everybody is safe.

FREEDOM IS SLAVERY is never fully explained in the novel. We are to assume that all Party members are living in a kind of slavery that frees them from having to make decisions.

IGNORANCE IS STRENGTH is explained at length in *Two*, *IX* and in the *Appendix*. The Party, we learn in *Two*, *IX*, in the second long extract from Goldstein's book, maintains power by keeping people ignorant both of the past and of other societies. What they don't know won't upset them. With no basis for comparison, they have no reason for discontent with the life the Party provides for them. The instrument for this is *Newspeak*, described at length in the *Appendix*. It is designed to limit the number of words people use, on the premise that if they can't express complicated thoughts they won't be able to have them.

Term Paper Ideas

The Novel

1. Is *1984* a prophetic novel or a logical extension of history as it was in 1948, the year the book was finished?

2. How did Soviet history influence the novel?

3. Is *1984* a political novel or is it really about the loneliness of the thinking man? Support your opinion.

Literary Topics

4. Write about *1984* as satire, giving examples of Orwell's humor.

5. How does Orwell use detail to get comic effect? You can use the Parsons family as an example.

6. What is the significance of the paperweight in the novel? What does it mean to Winston? To the design of the novel?

7. What is the purpose of Newspeak words in the novel?

8. Write about the function of memory and nostalgia in the novel, basing your discussion on Winston's thoughts about the past and the objects he collects.

9. How does Orwell exaggerate to make his point? Use the *proles* fighting over saucepans and Winston's job as examples.

The Party

10. How does the Party use revisionism to its own purposes? Why do the people believe the Party is telling the truth?

11. Write about the telescreens and their effect on people.

12. Who is Big Brother, and what is his function in society?

13. How is the society of *1984* like our society today?

14. How is the society of *1984* different from U.S. society and Soviet society today?

15. Could Big Brother take over in America? Why? Why not?

16. How does *1984* reflect the author's illness and depression?

17. What is the function of Goldstein's book in the novel?

18. The Goldstein book helps/hinders the story. Explain.

Winston

19. Who is Winston Smith? What makes him different from all the other Party members? Use examples from *Part One*.

20. Write about Winston Smith as a romantic idealist. Why is he dissatisfied with his life? Examples from *Part One*.

21. Look at Winston as an extension of George Orwell. Write about the ways in which they are similar.

22. Looking at George Orwell's life, point out the ways in which he and Winston are different, basing your discussion on *Part One* and The Author and His Times.

23. What is Winston's view of women, as reflected

through his attitude toward Julia? Take examples from *Part Two*.

24. What is Winston's view of motherhood, as reflected in his memory of the refugee mother saving her child? Of the prole mother? Of his own mother?

25. Talk about Winston's guilt towards his own mother, and how this affects his outlook.

26. What is the significance of Winston's dreams?

27. Is Winston a doomed hero with a death wish? Write about how he brings about his own downfall, using his diary and his love affair as evidence.

28. How could Winston have prevented his capture and punishment? Write about ways in which you think he could have escaped.

29. Write about Winston and Julia's love affair as an act of rebellion against the Party, beginning with his first dream about her.

30. What is Winston's view of sex? Describe it, using his own thoughts about his mother, about Julia, and about his marriage.

31. Is Winston's view of sex conditioned by attitudes of the 1940s? What were these attitudes? How do they differ from Winston's?

32. Describe Winston's attitude toward O'Brien before his capture. What is the attraction? How is this demonstrated in *Part Three?*

33. Why does Winston still like O'Brien after he is captured?

Other Characters

34. Write about Julia as Winston's love object. What does he admire about her?

35. Is Julia a witty realist or a corrupt featherbrain? Defend your position with reference to the text.

36. Describe Julia. How is she like Winston? How is she unlike him?

37. Write about Julia as a reflection of the author's views on women, using descriptions of her and events from his life.

38. Write about Julia as romantic heroine.

39. How does Julia contribute to Winston's downfall? Is it completely her fault?

40. What are the qualities in O'Brien that Winston admires?

41. Who is O'Brien, and what does he stand for? Write about him as representative of the upper class.

42. Write about O'Brien as Winston's doom, or destiny.

43. Is the true love affair in *1984* one of the mind, between Winston and O'Brien? If you think so, explain, with examples from *Part Three*.

44. What is the relationship between O'Brien and Winston after Winston's capture? Why does O'Brien want to make him perfect? Find quotations in *Part Three*.

45. Describe the scene with O'Brien in Room 101 and tell whether it works for you, and why.

46. Write about the Parsons family—the father, mother and children—as different types of Party members.

47. Relate the Parsons children and the Junior Spies to Nazism, and to the Hitler Youth, basing your discussion on your knowledge of both World War II and the novel.

48. Make a character study of Mrs. Parsons as innocent victim.

49. Why is Mr. Parsons so grateful to be captured? Explain. What is the significance of his attitude in relation to the novel?

50. Relate the story of Jones, Aronson and Rutherford to the Soviet party purges.

51. What does the story of Jones, Aronson and Rutherford mean to Winston? Describe the function of the Chestnut Tree Cafe.

Further Reading

CRITICAL WORKS

Calder, Jenni. *Chronicles of Conscience: A Study of George Orwell and Arthur Koestler*. London: Secker & Warburg. 1968. A useful look at literary sources for *1984*.

Crick, Bernard. *George Orwell: A Life*. New York: Little, Brown and Co., an Atlantic Monthly Press book, 1980. If you're only going to look at one biography of Orwell, this should be the one. It's recent, interesting and complete.

Fyvel, T.R. *George Orwell*. New York: Macmillan, 1982. This personal memoir tells about Orwell's broadcasting days.

Hammond, J.R. *A George Orwell Companion*. New York: St. Martin's Press, 1982. A guide to the novels, documentaries and essays, with a long section on *1984* and a useful key to characters and locations.

Hynes, Samuel, editor. *Twentieth Century Interpretations of 1984*. Englewood Cliffs, N.J.: Prentice-Hall. 1971 selected essays about the novel by British and American writers including some acquaintances of Orwell.

Kalechofsky, Roberta. *George Orwell: 1984*. New York: Frederick Ungar Publishing Co., 1983. Biographical criticism with chronology.

Lewis, Peter. *George Orwell: The Road to 1984*. New York: Harcourt, Brace and Jovanovich, 1981. This swiftly paced, illustrated book is easy to read and gives interesting biographical background leading to the writing of *1984*.

Sandison, Alan. *The Last Man in Europe: An Essay on George Orwell*. New York: Barnes and Noble, 1973.

Sperber, Murray. "Gazing into the Glass Paperweight: The Structure and Psychology of Orwell's *1984*," *Modern Fiction Studies*, Vol. 26, pp. 213–26, 1980.

Stansky, Peter, editor. *On Nineteen Eighty-Four*. New York: San Francisco: W.H. Freeman and Co., 1983. Essays about *1984* from all angles—political, sexual, ideological. A good range of Orwell criticism represented.

Stansky, Peter, and Abrahams, William. Orwell: *The Transformation*, and *The Unknown Orwell*. New York: A.A. Knopf, 1980. These volumes about Orwell's early life and work and his adult life up through the Spanish Civil War in 1937 are as good as anything available. They tell as much about Orwell as a person as anything written and leave the reader hoping the authors are busy on Vol. III.

Steinhoff, William. *George Orwell and the Origins of 1984*. Ann Arbor: The University of Michigan Press, 1975. This is an academic critic's scholarly book, but it does trace the background of Goldstein's book in *1984* thoroughly, along with other literary influences on the novel.

Williams, Raymond. *George Orwell*. New York: Columbia University Press, 1971. A look at Orwell's responses to English society.

AUTHOR'S OTHER WORKS

Orwell, George.   *Animal Farm*. New York: Harcourt, Brace and Jovanovich, 1954.

————.   *Burmese Days*. New York: Harcourt, Brace and Jovanovich, 1950.

————.   *Clergyman's Daughter*. New York: Harcourt, Brace and Jovanovich, 1969.

————.   *Collected Essays, Journalism and Letters*, Vol. I: *An Age Like This*. New York: Harcourt, Brace and Jovanovich, 1971.

————.   *Collected Essays*, . . . Vol. II: *My Country Right or Left*. New York: Harcourt, Brace and Jovanovich, 1971.

————.   *Collected Essays*, . . . Vol. III: *As I Please*. New York: Harcourt, Brace and Jovanovich, 1971.

————.   *Collected Essays*, . . . Vol. IV: *In Front of Your Nose*. New York: Harcourt, Brace and Jovanovich, 1971.

————.   *Collection of Essays*. New York: Harcourt, Brace and Jovanovich, 1970.

————.   *Coming up for Air*. New York: Harcourt, Brace and Jovanovich, 1969.

————.   *Dickens, Dali and Others*. New York: Harcourt, Brace and Jovanovich, 1970.

————.   *Down and Out in Paris and London*. New York: Harcourt, Brace and Jovanovich, 1972.

————.   *The English People*. London: Haskell. 1974.

————.   *Homage to Catalonia*. New York: Harcourt, Brace and Jovanovich, 1969.

————.   *Keep the Aspidistra Flying*. New York: Harcourt, Brace and Jovanovich, 1969.

————.   *The Orwell Reader: Fiction, Essays, and Reportage*. New York: Harcourt, Brace and Jovanovich, 1961.

————.   *The Road to Wigan Pier*. New York: Harcourt, Brace and Jovanovich.

Glossary

Doublethink To hold two contradictory opinions, knowing they are contradictory and believing in both.

Eastasia One of the three superpowers in the world, consisting of China, Japan, Manchuria, Mongolia and Tibet. Sometimes at war with Oceania.

Eurasia Another superpower, made up of all northern Europe and western Asia. Sometimes at war with Oceania, where Winston Smith lives.

Hate Week Week in which Oceanian citizens all attend rallies and parades to inflame hatred of Party enemies and heighten their efforts on behalf of Oceania.

INGSOC The name of the Party that rules Oceania, where Winston lives. Name taken from English Socialism, a form of government in England, which Orwell exaggerated and pushed to the limits of his imagination. Writing the novel, Orwell made it plain he was not attacking English Socialism as it existed in 1948–9.

Julia The dark-haired rebellious Party member Winston loves.

Newspeak Official language of the Party.

O'Brien A powerful Inner Party member who is either Winston's best friend, worst enemy or both.

Oceania Superstate in which Winston Smith lives. Made up of the Americas and the Atlantic islands, including the British Isles, Australia, and the southern portion of Africa. Always at war with one or both of the other superstates.

Ownlife Individuality or eccentricity.

Proles Short for proletarians, the uneducated common people.

Telescreen Giant screen in every public and private place that both transmits Party propaganda and entertainment, and keeps an eye on Party members, looking for traces of *Thoughtcrime.*

Thoughtcrime   Thinking anything not approved by the Party. Anyone apprehended for *thoughtcrime* will be vaporized.

Thought Police   Corps assigned to arresting people guilty of *Thoughtcrime.*

Unperson   A criminal who has been purged and therefore ceases to exist. The person has been removed from the Party and perhaps even vaporized and removed from history through changes in written records.

Vaporized   Fate of enemies of the Party. The person disappears, only Big Brother knows how.

Victory Cigarettes/Gin/Mansions   The Party gives these names to inferior products to make them seem more attractive.

The Critics

Orwell and Eric Blair

The creation of George Orwell was an act of will by Eric Blair, and it was carried on at almost every level of his existence, affecting not only his prose style but also the style of his daily life. Becoming George Orwell was his way of making himself into a writer, at which he brilliantly succeeded, and of unmaking himself as a gentleman, of opting out of the genteel lower-upper middle class into which he was born, at which he had only an equivocal success . . . it allowed Eric Blair to come to terms with his world.

> —Peter Stansky and William Abrahams, *Orwell: The Transformation*, 1979–80

A Warning Against Totalitarianism

Nineteen Eighty-Four is a long premeditated, rational warning against totalitarian tendencies in societies like our own rather than a sick and sudden prophecy about a Soviet or neo-Nazi takeover, still less a scream of despair and recantation of his democratic Socialism. Its harsh style created as authentic a picture of a state turned by men themselves into hell as the lyrical passages of *Animal Farm* give a picture of a natural, pastoral and egalitarian Utopia. . . . *Nineteen Eighty-Four* may show sociological rather than psychological imagination, but imagination of a high order none the less.

> —Bernard Crick, *George Orwell: A Life*, 1980

If *Nineteen Eighty-Four* is treated as a warning rather than a prophecy, as a satire on present tendencies rather than a forecast of the future, it can be seen that its effect has been totally salutary. Today such terms as 'doublethink', 'newspeak' and 'thoughtcrime' have passed into accepted usage and for a generation of readers the book has come to be regarded as a standard treatise on the growth and influence of totalitarian trends. . . .

—J.R. Hammond, *A George Orwell Companion*, 1982

In previous writings he had stressed that bourgeois individuality was going, the bonds of family, locality, religion, craft and profession were going. In their place a new collectivism was spreading in society. . . . But it also appeared to Orwell in 1948 that the new collective did not bring the earthly paradise any nearer. Not only that, it appeared to him that under the threat of violence and nuclear terror, the new collective could become grotesquely dehumanized. It is as a permanent warning against the danger of the dehumanized collective in our society that *Nineteen Eighty-Four* has survived. . . .

—T.R. Fyvel, *George Orwell*, 1982

Orwell and the Lower Classes

Winston Smith holds up the Proles, not too convincingly, as 'the only hope' for the future. But Orwell, even in tramp's clothing, never pretended to be a Prole. He remained always aware of the gulf between him and the class he envied. Did he like them? It is hard to be sure he did. His aim was to be personally as classless as possible.

—Peter Lewis, *George Orwell: The Road to 1984*

Orwell and Winston Smith

Winston Smith's sensibility, then, can be seen as representing a constellation of special intellectual, aesthetic, and literary values. There is the love of what Newspeak calls *oldthink*, that is, the ideas grouped round the equally outmoded concepts of 'objectivity and rationalism' and of old folk rhymes. There is, further, his love of the particular

and the detailed in other things. . . . Behind these
aspects of Winston's inner sense of values is the
larger idea that individual feeling is the most
essential and desirable reality available.

> —Ian Watt, "Winston Smith: The
> Last Humanist," in *On Nineteen
> Eighty-Four*, ed. Peter Stansky,
> 1983

Throughout his career, Orwell had two themes
that he made particularly his own: first, the experience of impoverishment—not of poverty, to
which many are born, but of the fall into poverty
by those not bred to cope with it—and second, the
political obligation of the intellectual class to maintain steadfast loyalty to the cause of truth. The figure of Winston Smith combines both these
themes. He is one with a number of earlier figures
in Orwell's novels who have their economic pins
knocked out and become conscious of the slummy
underside of industrial civilization. . . . He lives in
an imaginary world, in which the 'middling' intellectual class has been stripped of the protection of
money by a stroke of their author's pen.

> —Alvin C. Kibel, *Papers, International
> Orwell Conference*

Orwell on Women

We have seen that the roles assigned to women
in Oceania and in Winston Smith's mind fall into
very limited stereotypes: the pure self-sacrificing
mother, the frigid wife, the sexually aggressive
and emotionally supportive mate. We must now
ask whether there is a 'hidden agenda' for women
in this anti-Utopian book. Does George Orwell in
any way imply that women in an ideal world
should be different? The answer I fear is No. From
the perspective of a feminist living in 1984, Orwell's attitude toward women and the family is
discouragingly conservative and repressive. However brilliantly Orwell foretold the horrors of total-

itarian thinking and political control, he failed to see that embedded in his own attitudes toward women was an ideology almost as oppressive to the female as the Party is to Smith.

—Anne Mellor, " 'You're Only a Rebel from the Waist Downwards': Orwell's View of Women," in *Nineteen Eighty-Four*, ed. Peter Stansky, 1983

Orwell and O'Brien

O'Brien's explanation of his conduct and that of the other members of the Inner Party is not irrational; it is the conduct that is irrational, and his creator knew it was. That an insane murderer may understand why he murders neither prevents what he does nor makes the crime less horrifying. It is too bad that Orwell's beliefs have at times been confused with O'Brien's, for this has prevented some readers from seeing how profoundly Orwell understood totalitarianism. . . . The long dialogue between O'Brien and Smith demonstrates Orwell's awareness that implicit in totalitarianism is a desire for expansion—physical, intellectual, spiritual—that . . . recognizes no limits.

—William Steinhoff, *George Orwell and the Origins of 1984*